THE
PASSION
TRANSLATION

THE PASSIONATE LIFE BIBLE STUDY SERIES

12-LESSON STUDY GUIDE

THE BOOK OF
MATTHEW

OUR LOVING KING

BroadStreet
PUBLISHING

BroadStreet Publishing® Group, LLC
Savage, Minnesota, USA
BroadStreetPublishing.com

TPT: The Book of Matthew: 12-Lesson Study Guide
Copyright © 2023 BroadStreet Publishing Group

9781424564392 (softcover)
9781424564408 (e-book)

Stock or custom editions of BroadStreet Publishing titles may be purchased in bulk for educational, business, ministry, fundraising, or sales promotional use. For information, please email orders@broadstreetpublishing.com.

General editor: Brian Simmons
Managing editor: William D. Watkins
Writer: Andrew P. Kauth

Design and typesetting by Garborg Design Works | garborgdesign.com

Printed in China

23 24 25 26 27 5 4 3 2 1

Contents

From God's Heat to Yours

"God is love," says the apostle John, and "Everyone who loves is fathered by God and experiences an intimate knowledge of him" (1 John 4:7). The life of a Christ-follower is, at its core, a life of love—God's love of us, our love of him, and our love of others and ourselves because of God's love for us.

And this divine love is reliable, trustworthy, unconditional, other-centered, majestic, forgiving, redemptive, patient, kind, and more precious than anything else we can ever receive or give. It characterizes each person of the Trinity—Father, Son, and Holy Spirit—and so is as limitless as they are. They love one another with this eternal love, and they reach beyond themselves to us, created in their image with this love.

How do we know such incredible truths? Through the primary source of all else we know about the one God—his Word, the Bible. Of course, God reveals who he is through other sources as well, such as the natural world, miracles, our inner life, our relationships (especially with him), those who minister on his behalf, and those who proclaim him to us and others. But the fullest and most comprehensive revelation we have of God and from him is what he has given us in the thirty-nine books of the Hebrew Scriptures (the Old Testament) and the twenty-seven books of the Christian Scriptures (the New Testament). Together, these sixty-six books present a compelling and telling portrait of God and his dealings with us.

It is these Scriptures that *The Passionate Life Bible Study Series* is all about. Through these study guides, we—the editors and writers of this series—seek to provide you with a unique and welcoming opportunity to delve more deeply into God's precious Word, encountering there his loving heart for you and all the others he loves. God wants you to know him more deeply, to love him more devoutly, and to share his heart with others more frequently and freely. To accomplish this, we have based this study guide series on The Passion Translation of the Bible, which strives to "reintroduce the passion and fire of the Bible to the English reader. It doesn't merely convey the literal meaning of words. It expresses God's passion for people and his world by translating the original, life-changing message of God's Word for modern readers." It has been created to "kindle in you a burning desire to know the heart of God, while impacting the church for years to come."[1]

In each study guide, you will find an introduction to the Bible book it covers. There you will gain information about that Bible book's authorship, date of composition, first recipients, setting, purpose, central message, and key themes. Each lesson following the introduction will take a portion of that Bible book and walk you through it so you will learn its content better while experiencing and applying God's heart for your own life and encountering ways you can share his heart with others. Along the way, you will come across a number of features we have created that provide opportunities for more life application and growth in biblical understanding.

 ## Experience God's Heart

This feature focuses questions on personal application. It will help you live out God's Word and to bring the Bible into your world in fresh, exciting, and relevant ways.

 ## Share God's Heart

This feature will help you grow in your ability to share with other people what you learn and apply in a given lesson. It provides guidance on using the lesson to grow closer to others and to enrich your fellowship with others. It also points the way to enabling you to better listen to the stories of others so you can bridge the biblical story with their stories.

The Backstory

This feature provides ancient historical and cultural background that illuminates Bible passages and teachings. It deals with then-pertinent religious groups, communities, leaders, disputes, business trades, travel routes, customs, nations, political factions, ancient measurements and currency...in short, anything historical or cultural that will help you better understand what Scripture says and means.

 Word Wealth

This feature provides definitions for and other illuminating information about key terms, names, and concepts, and how different ancient languages have influenced the biblical text. It also provides insight into the different literary forms in the Bible, such as prophecy, poetry, narrative history, parables, and letters, and how knowing the form of a text can help you better interpret and apply it. Finally, this feature highlights the most significant passages in a Bible book. You may be encouraged to memorize these verses or keep them before you in some way so you can actively hide God's Word in your heart.

 Digging Deeper

This feature explains the theological significance of a text or the controversial issues that arise and mentions resources you can use to help you arrive at your own conclusions. Another way to dig deeper into the Word is by looking into the life of a biblical character or another person from church history, showing how that man or woman incarnated a biblical truth or passage. For instance, Jonathan Edwards was well known for his missions work among native American Indians and for his intellectual prowess in articulating the Christian faith, Florence Nightingale for the reforms she brought about in healthcare, Irenaeus for his fight against heresy, Billy Graham for his work in evangelism, Moses for the strength God gave him to lead the Hebrews and receive and communicate the law, and Deborah for her work as a judge in Israel. This feature introduces to you figures from the past who model what it looks like to experience God's heart and share his heart with others.

The Extra Mile

While The Passion Translation's notes are extensive, sometimes students of Scripture like to explore more on their own. In this feature, we provide you with opportunities to glean more information from a Bible dictionary, a Bible encyclopedia, a reliable Bible online tool, another ancient text, and the like. Here you will learn how you can go the extra mile on a Bible lesson. And not just in study either. Reflection, prayer, discussion, and applying a passage in new ways provide even more opportunities to go the extra mile. Here you will find questions to answer and applications to make that will require more time and energy from you—if and when you have them to give.

As you can see above, each of these features has a corresponding icon so you can quickly and easily identify them.

You will find other helps and guidance through the lessons of these study guides, including thoughtful questions, application suggestions, and spaces for you to record your own reflections, answers, and action steps. Of course, you can also write in your own journal, notebook, computer document, or other resource, but we have provided you with space for your convenience.

Also, each lesson will direct you toward the introductory material and numerous notes provided in The Passion Translation. There each Bible book contains a number of aids supplied to help you better grasp God's words and his incredible love, power, knowledge, plans, and so much more. We want you to get the most out of your Bible study, especially using it to draw you closer to the One who loves you most.

Finally, at the end of each lesson you'll find a section called "Talking It Out." This contains questions and exercises for application that you can share, answer, and apply with your spouse, a friend, a coworker, a Bible study group, or any other individuals or groups who would like to walk with you through this material. As Christians, we gather together to serve, study, worship, sing, evangelize, and a host of other activities. We grow together, not just on our own. This section will give you ample opportunities to engage others with some of the content of each lesson so you can work it out in community.

We offer all of this to support you in becoming an even more faithful and loving disciple of Jesus Christ. A disciple in the ancient world was a student of her teacher, a follower of his master. Students study, and followers follow. Jesus' disciples are to sit at his feet and listen and learn and then do what he tells them and shows them to do. We have created *The Passionate Life Bible Study Series* to help you do what a disciple of Jesus is called to do.

So go.

Read God's words.

Hear what he has to say in them and through them.

Meditate on them.

Hide them in your heart.

Display their truths in your life.

Share their truths with others.

Let them ignite Jesus' passion and light in all you say and do.

Use them to help you fulfill what Jesus called his disciples to do: "Now wherever you go, make disciples of all nations, baptizing them in the name of the Father, the Son, and the Holy Spirit. And teach them to faithfully follow all that I have commanded you. And never forget that I am with you every day, even to the completion of this age" (Matthew 28:19–20).

And through all of this, let Jesus' love nourish your heart and allow that love to overflow into your relationships with others (John 15:9–13). For it was for love that Jesus came, served, died, rose from the dead, and ascended into heaven. This love he gives us. And this love he wants us to pass along to others.

Why I Love the Book of Matthew

We are so blessed to have four Gospels to present four glimpses into the life, words, and works of Jesus Christ. We cherish each one: Matthew, Mark, Luke, and John. Taken together, these books covering Jesus' life present to us the true gospel—the good news that sets people free.

Every time I read Matthew's Gospel, I am challenged with the truths of the kingdom of heaven. Matthew pulls no punches. The words of his Gospel penetrate the heart of all who read his masterpiece. Written from a clearly Jewish perspective, the former tax collector is precise and potent. No one can read the book of Matthew and not ponder deeply the man from Galilee and the message of his life. Jesus Christ stands triumphant in this book! I love Matthew because it challenges me to go further in my faith commitment to follow the Lamb of God.

The message of Matthew is clear: Jesus is King, and he is bringing his kingdom to the earth. Every chapter of Matthew makes the case that there is only one Savior, a Messiah who came to set us free from our past—our self-life with its shame and guilt. Jesus is revealed as the hope of the broken hearted, the healer of the sick, and the helper of the weak and outcast. Truly, he is the friend of sinners. The writer and disciple Matthew knows, for he was brought out of his compromised past into the privilege of being with Jesus and hearing firsthand the words of the Son of Man. I love the book of Matthew, for it shows me how tender and considerate is our Savior. Matthew shares with us Jesus' kind invitation: "Learn my ways and you'll discover that I'm gentle, humble, easy to please" (Matthew 11:29).

It is amazing how often Jesus was opposed and maligned by those who thought they were serving God. Religion had blinded the Pharisees and scribes from seeing the one who stood before them. The powers that be likewise had no clue that the Son of Man was in their midst. He was a political and religious outcast, yet still he remained faithful to the Father to complete his mission of bringing salvation to the world. I love Matthew because of how he demonstrates the great courage and faithful heart of Jesus. Our King was not intimidated by those who opposed him or simply wanted to debate with him. In spite of it all, Jesus remained pure in heart, unmoved, and unshakable.

When I went into the studio to record the audiobook version of Matthew, I wept more than once. Reading through the book stirred my soul. When I got to Chapter 28 and the grand finale of the resurrection of Jesus Christ, I couldn't hold back my tears. Our King is a champion. He defeated every argument, every sickness, every storm, and every enemy, and he emerged triumphant from the grave. Our King is a resurrected prince. I love Matthew because I see a King, my King, who is returning one day to reveal to the nations how great he is and to break every bondage from the human heart as far as the curse is found. Join me now in studying this monumental account of the life and works of Jesus Christ, our King.

Brian Simmons
General Editor

LESSON 1

King Jesus

(Matthew 1–2)

Matthew's Gospel begins the New Testament and leads the four Gospels (Matthew, Mark, Luke, and John). It is a fitting start to the second part of the Bible and serves well as a natural bridge between the Old and New Testaments. Why? Because Matthew's Gospel clearly demonstrates that a new age is at hand, an age of the fulfillment of God's promise of a Savior for his people.

The book of Matthew, then, is truly good news, what Jesus calls the "joyful message of God's kingdom realm" (Matthew 9:35). Matthew, from the onset of his Gospel, establishes a clear purpose: the demonstration that the promised Messiah has arrived. Moreover, he reveals that Jesus is that Messiah—the loving King of that heavenly kingdom realm. And Matthew details throughout his writings that Jesus has prescribed something new for humanity, namely service to him, their loving King, by first loving God and then loving their neighbors.

From the miracles Jesus performs to the mysteries revealed through the parables he tells and the teachings he imparts, Matthew confidently shows his readers exactly who Jesus is. He is the Old Testament promise fulfilled, the one to whom our salvation is owed. Through Matthew's detailed genealogy of Jesus and the descriptions of Jesus' miraculous birth to his death and resurrection, Matthew records all that is necessary to secure the knowledge that Jesus is, truly, the "pioneer and perfecter faith" (Hebrews 12:2 NIV).

Authorship

Similar to the other four Gospels, Matthew lacks a true "about the author" section; like the other Gospels, this one does not specify who wrote it. However, church tradition names Matthew as the author. Eusebius of Caesarea, the famous church historian of the fourth century, quotes Papias, a church leader who knew and heard the apostle John say that Matthew wrote the Gospel attributed to him.[2] And while little is known about Matthew the man, he is traditionally considered to be the famous tax collector, the one who became one of Jesus' twelve apostles (Matthew 9:9–13; 10:3). Mark and Luke also refer to Matthew using the name Levi (Mark 2:13–17; Luke 5:27–31).

- *Have you ever switched careers? Maybe you've moved from one company to another. How did the change make you feel? Full of hope? Excited? Uncertain? Full of fear? How do you think Matthew felt about leaving behind his life as a tax collector to follow Jesus?*

- *Prior to knowing Jesus, what was your life like? Matthew was likely well off financially but despised by his fellow Jews for being a tax collector, and he may have abused his position for his own financial gain. How might Matthew have felt relating to the other apostles/disciples of Jesus? To the countless people he met as he followed Jesus throughout the years of Jesus' ministry?*

Date and Audience

The book of Matthew is commonly dated between AD 55 to the mid-60s, though some scholars place the writing of Matthew after AD 70. The predominant modern theory of Matthew's date of origin is known as the two-source theory, which expands upon the notion that the book of Matthew may have been penned within a few years after Jesus' death and resurrection and relies upon two written sources in addition to Matthew's own firsthand experiences as one of Jesus' closest followers. These other two sources are the Gospel of Mark and a collection of sayings of Jesus known as "Q."[3] The significance here is that Matthew was a contemporary of the other Gospel authors and, even more significantly, one of Jesus' closest followers.

Now, just as debate exists surrounding the actual date of composition, a debate also surrounds the book of Matthew's language of origin, with most scholars citing church tradition and agreeing that the original language of the Gospel of Matthew was Hebrew. It certainly makes sense to hold this opinion as Matthew, a Jewish man, wrote with a Jewish audience in mind. The text itself reveals this in numerous ways; for example, Matthew repeatedly shows that Jesus came to fulfill the law (Matthew 5:17–20) and provide a new "law" or way (the Sermon on the Mount), which Jesus confirmed by his many miracles.

- *Read Matthew 1:1–17. Why did Matthew include, especially at the outset, a lineage that traces Jesus' ancestry all the way back to Abraham? Who was Abraham, and what would be the significance of following Jesus' lineage back to him (see Genesis 12:1–3; 17:1–8)?*

- *Matthew also traces Jesus' genealogy to David, once the king of Israel. Why would showing this about Jesus' heritage be important (see 2 Samuel 7:16; Psalm 89:20–29; Jeremiah 33:14–22)?*

Major Themes

Matthew's Gospel has five major themes, which are detailed in the "Introduction" to Matthew in *The Passion Translation*. After reading about these themes, answer the questions that follow.

- ***Gospel-telling.*** *The book of Matthew contains an exciting story, namely the good news that the Son of God has arrived, that he had a miraculous conception, taught heavenly sanctioned truths, and died and rose from the dead according to prophecies embedded in the Old Testament. Read Matthew 1:18–21. In what ways were Jesus' conception and birth unlike any other human's?*

- ***Old Testament.*** *After proving Jesus' kingly lineage from David, Matthew continues to demonstrate that Jesus is the promised Messiah. For Matthew, it's vital that he include many references to the fulfillment of Old Testament prophesies and promises. For example, read Matthew 1:22–23 and 2:5–6. How does Jesus fulfill the prophesies found in Isaiah 7:14 and Micah 5:2?*

- **Parables.** Matthew details twelve parables in his Gospel. For Matthew, these allegorical stories explain the mysteries revealed in the person and teachings of Jesus. They detail the life of the kingdom of heaven. What is your favorite parable? What lesson does it teach, and how does that lesson encourage you in your daily life?

- **Heavenly kingdom realm.** Jesus did not necessarily bring the kingdom that he was expected to bring. He had no intention of staging a military takeover in order to free the Jewish people from Roman rule. Rather, he brought the keys to an eternal kingdom. Did you ever receive a very small gift when you were expecting something much larger only to open it and find a clue leading you to a much more extravagant gift? Can you remember a time when your expectations were seemingly not met only to realize later that what you eventually received was well beyond your initial expectations?

- *Kingdom realm living.* *The book of Matthew is rich with instruction for the followers of Jesus, with submission to King Jesus at the heart of it all. How does Joseph demonstrate obedience on two separate occasions in the first two chapters of Matthew? How did the famed "wise men" demonstrate obedience to God (2:1–12)?*

♥ EXPERIENCE GOD'S HEART

Take some time to read through the entire Gospel of Matthew. As you read through the story of Jesus in this book, reflect on your own hopes and dreams. Just as *The Passion Translation* seeks to ignite your passion for reading the Bible, so Jesus seeks to win the passions of your heart. His mission? To seek and save the lost.

- *What would you say was Jesus' mission during his earthly ministry? What was he striving to accomplish and for whom?*

- *Now what would you say is your life mission? What do you hope to accomplish and for whom?*

- *How does your mission line up with Jesus'? How is yours different from his? How is it similar to his mission? Write down your thoughts.*

♥ SHARE GOD'S HEART

Good news should be shared! Matthew and the apostles gave up everything to follow Jesus. They left careers, homes, and family. Most gave up their very lives, including Matthew, who, according to Christian tradition, suffered a painful martyrdom, which may have included being tied to a cross, stoned, and then beheaded.[4]

We love to tell our family and friends about all the good things that happen in life. A quick phone call or text makes that so easy. And we often run to social media to post about everything that is happening in our lives: from a great party to an awesome gift to a major purchase. Matthew wasn't that much different in that respect. He told others about Jesus and wrote down an account of Jesus' life, death, and resurrection.

- *Take a few minutes to write out a list of those people in your life with whom you'd like to share the good news of Jesus. Even if you aren't at a place where you feel bold enough to share with those who don't yet know the love of Jesus, writing out a quick top ten list will help encourage you. Whether a family member, a friend, a neighbor, or a coworker, as you write their names, pray about an opportunity to share with them what you already know to be true: Jesus loves you, and he is ready to be your King!*

Talking It Out

Since Christians grow in community, not just in solitude, here are some questions you may want to discuss with another person or in a group. Each "Talking It Out" section is designed with this purpose in mind.

1. While one of the main purposes of the book of Matthew is to reveal the true nature of Jesus and to share his story with the Jewish people, the author is also writing to us. What parts of Jesus' story mean the most to you? Why?

2. Jesus is truly our loving King. Jesus was born, lived, died, and rose from the dead for you. Remember that one of the themes of Matthew is "kingdom realm living." How can you better live out a kingdom-centered life? What areas of your life might you need to surrender to Jesus? Or what aspects of your daily life could use a bit of kingdom refinement?

3. Among the four Gospels, Matthew shows more than the others how Jesus' life, death, and resurrection fulfilled prophecies found in the Old Testament. Why do you think emphasizing this might have mattered to Matthew's initial readers, first-century Jews? What significance do you think those fulfilled prophecies could have for many people today?

LESSON 2

True Repentance

(Matthew 3–4)

According to Billy Graham, *repentance* is a word of power and action that involves three elements: conviction, contrition, and change. Further he stated that "it is an act that breaks the chains of captive sinners and sets heaven to singing."[5] In other words, repentance doesn't involve just saying that you're sorry. True repentance involves real life change.

When John the Baptizer started preaching, his message was simple: "Heaven's kingdom is about to appear—so you'd better keep turning away from evil and turn back to God!" (Matthew 3:2). John called for real change, a turning back to God. "You must prove your repentance by a changed life," he preached (v. 8).

🅝 WORD WEALTH

In Matthew 3:2, John implores his listeners to turn away from evil and turn back to God. The literal meaning of the Hebrew word for "repent" is *teshuvah*, meaning "return." The implication here is that sin causes a person to stray from God whereas a person's duty is to be with God. The only way to be with God, then, is to turn from one's sinful ways. The Greek word carries a similar connotation. The Greek word for "repent" is *metanoeo*, which literally means "to think differently" or "to perceive afterward."

It signifies a changing of one's mind or purpose. But, as New Testament scholar D. A. Carson points out, the biblical use of "repent" includes more than an intellectual change in outlook: "What is meant is not a merely intellectual change of mind or mere grief, still less doing penance..., but a radical transformation of the entire person, a fundamental turnaround involving mind and action and including overtones of grief, which results in 'fruit in keeping with repentance.'"[6]

- *Was there a time in your life where you made a decision to turn from a particular sin and turn back to God? A time where you had to change your mind, your heart, and your ways? Tell about it here.*

- *Share your experience with a family member or friend whom you see in a similar situation or who might benefit from your story in another way.*

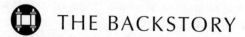 THE BACKSTORY

What's in a name? In the case of John the Baptizer, a lot! The third chapter of Matthew introduces John as a rather wild sort of man. He wore clothing made of camel's hair, lived in the desert, and had a diet that was primarily dried locusts and honey (3:4). John's name means "YAHWEH has graced him," and he was also known as John the Immerser, due to the manner in which he baptized those who confessed their sins after hearing him preach.[7] We are able to learn even more about John in Luke 1, where further details reveal that he was a cousin of Jesus and the son of a priest. An angel revealed to his father, Zechariah, that John would be a great prophet and would prepare the way for the coming Messiah:

> He will go before the Lord as a forerunner,
> with the same power and anointing as
> Elijah the prophet. He will be instrumental
> in turning the hearts of the fathers in
> tenderness back to their children and
> the hearts of the disobedient back to the
> wisdom of their righteous fathers. And he
> will prepare a united people who are ready
> for the Lord's appearing. (Luke 1:17).

- *Read Luke 1:5–25, 76–77, which provide the story about the conception of John and what he would do for his family and Israel. Jot down what you learn about John.*

- *What does your name mean? If you don't know, a quick online search will give you some insight. Were you given your name for a specific reason (named after a relative or named by your parents due to a specific revelation from God)? Is the meaning of your name significant to you? Does it describe you in an accurate way? Why or why not?*

- *Why did Jesus require someone to go before him to prepare the way for him? What was the significance of John the Baptizer's ministry? Hint: Read Matthew 11:11–19 and consider what John realized that most others did not.*

Temptation

After being baptized by John, Jesus went into the wilderness by himself. Weak and hungry after a forty-day fast, Jesus stood face-to-face with Satan, the accuser, who sought to challenge Jesus' authority and power. We can learn a lot from the way in which Jesus confronted temptation. He faced each lie with a verse from Deuteronomy. For example, when challenged to turn stones into bread, Jesus simply replied that "bread alone will not satisfy" (see Deuteronomy 8:3). Read the account of Jesus being tempted in Matthew 4:1–11.

- *What were the second and third temptations that Jesus faced? What verse from Deuteronomy did he use to speak truth when confronted with a lie?*

- *After going without food for well over a month, Jesus was understandably worn down, yet he remained focused on God and his mission. Have you ever fasted? If so, why did you decide to fast, and how long did your fast last? How did you feel physically after fasting? If you fasted for spiritual reasons, did your experience of fasting result in a greater reliance upon God or on any particular revelation from God? Why or why not?*

♥ EXPERIENCE GOD'S HEART

After angels attended to Jesus following his ordeal in the wilderness, he moved his ministry from Nazareth to Capernaum and began preaching his message: "Keep turning away from your sins and come back to God, for heaven's kingdom realm is now accessible" (v. 17). God's heart for each of us is to repent and return. And in the midst of that, he finds us and calls us to himself.

- *The first followers Jesus called were fishermen. When Jesus called them, they left immediately. They left everything: their nets, their boats, and their families. Where were you when you felt God calling you? What was your situation at the time? Describe this period in your life and what God's call meant to you.*

♥ SHARE GOD'S HEART

Jesus healed many people as he ministered. He healed those who were in pain and those who suffered from all kinds of illnesses and infirmities, from epilepsy and paralysis to demonic possession. Because of all the healing and because so many were set free, Jesus became well known and massive crowds followed him (v. 25).

As followers of Jesus, we have the power to heal the sick as well. In fact, Jesus says the following in Matthew 10:8: "You must continually bring healing to lepers and to those who are sick, and make it your habit to break off the demonic presence from people, and raise the dead back to life. Freely you have received the power of the kingdom, so freely release it to others." Whom do you know who needs a touch from Jesus? Maybe it's as simple as an encouraging word, or maybe it's more complicated and they need healing from cancer or some other horrible illness. Ask God to put someone on your heart and then reach out to him or her with a phone call, a text, a letter, or even a personal visit.

Talking It Out

1. John the Baptizer lived an interesting life. He preached in the wilderness, dressed wildly, and ate a rather bizarre diet. Why was his lifestyle so necessary? Would he have been as effective if he had dressed like his contemporaries and preached in the city?

2. Where is God calling you to share the gospel message? How can you faithfully go about accomplishing God's purposes for your life in your cultural setting?

3. Jesus had John baptize him. At first John was hesitant and told Jesus it should be the other way around, with Jesus baptizing him. What did Jesus mean in Matthew 3:15 when he said, "It is only right to do all that God requires"? How did God honor Jesus in this moment? And what might God be requiring of you as you follow his Son?

4. Have you been baptized as an adult? If so, what did that moment mean for you? If you are a Christ-follower and have not been baptized, discuss baptism with a friend, your small group, or your pastor. Are you ready to be baptized? Why or why not?

LESSON 3

The Sermon on the Hillside

The Blessed

(Matthew 5:1–16)

Chapters 5–7 of the book of Matthew contain Jesus' longest continued discourse, typically referred to as the Sermon on the Mount. Indeed, these three chapters cover Jesus' most concrete teachings, teachings that every follower of Jesus should seek to put at the center of his or her Christian walk. And Jesus does not hesitate to set an extraordinarily high standard, with instructions that his followers cannot, for example, "hold anger in [their] heart toward a fellow believer, [or they will be] subject to judgment" (5:22) or to "love your enemy, bless the one who curses you, do something wonderful for the one who hates you" (v. 44). Glen Stassen and David Gushee note that "Jesus taught that the test of our discipleship is whether we act on his teachings, whether we 'put into practice' his words."[8]

 THE BACKSTORY

It is relevant to point out that Jesus' famed Sermon on the Hillside has a parallel account in the book of Luke, a message typically referred to as the Sermon on the Plain (see Luke 6:17–49).

The fact that Luke records this occasion allows for the conclusion that the message of Jesus' sermon was likely delivered in varying forms on several different occasions. And while some scholars hold that Matthew and Luke recorded the same sermon, Luke clearly omits material contained in Matthew's account. In fact, Matthew's account is quite extensive, comparatively; Matthew's version contains 107 verses to Luke's 30.[9] It is quite easy, therefore, and certainly valid, to form a position that the Sermon on the Mount contained in the book of Matthew is an anthology, a collection of Jesus' teachings combined to form an ethical sermon representative of how and what he preached. And while it is necessary to point out the varying opinions on whether the Sermon on the Mount was one sermon or a collection of teachings, it is even more important to consider Jesus' audience, his purpose for the sermon, and the variety of interpretations of Jesus' words.

Overview

In the case of the Sermon on the Mount, Jesus was directing his teachings to his disciples, his followers. Matthew states that Jesus' "followers and disciples [were] spread over the hillside" (5:1). The purpose of Matthew 5–7 is to inform those who believe in him concerning the true reality of following him, what that journey looks like, and what he expects of those loyal to him. To that point, the words of Jesus left them all "awestruck" (7:28). Why? Because it was as challenging then as it is today. The Sermon on the Mount tells believers that they must be different, that they must be "salt and light" (5:13–14).

• *Read Matthew 5–7 at least once all the way through.*

- *Now jot down some of your impressions of what Jesus taught. Include any questions you have.*

- *The Sermon on the Mount contains many teachings that are quite challenging: anger is paramount to hate, lust is adultery in your heart, etc. List two of the teachings from the Sermon on the Mount that you feel are particularly challenging.*

- *How might applying these teachings in your own life be a challenge? And how will a true application of these teachings in your life see a greater transformation of your heart? Jesus' sermon is not as much about outward duty as inward transformation.*

A quick internet search will result in no less than half a dozen ways to interpret the Sermon on the Hillside: the social gospel view, the view that it is merely an elaboration of the Mosaic law, the dispensational view, and so on. D. Martyn Lloyd-Jones, who served for many years as minister of Westminster Chapel in London, England, wrote one of the more well-known studies of the Sermon on the Hillside. He states that the reason Christians should study it and try to live by its precepts is simply because "the Lord Jesus Christ died to enable us to live the Sermon on the Mount."[10] Lloyd-Jones goes further and provides several reasons Christians should study Matthew 5–7: it shows the absolute need for the gospel and its grace, it produces an abundance of blessing when you live it out, and it is the best means of evangelism.[11]

- *Read Titus 2:14. Paul, the apostle who knew the grace of God so well in his own life, says that Jesus died "to purify for himself a people who are his very own, passionate to do what is beautiful in his eyes." How do you view the Sermon on the Mount? Do you view it as something that is an unattainable standard? Or perhaps you regard it as a simple code of ethics or morals? Or do you feel that the Sermon on the Mount is to be read, applied, and lived out with God's transforming grace and power?*

The Beatitudes

Jesus begins the Sermon on the Hillside without asking anything and without giving any instruction. Rather, he lists a series of conditions and results known as the Beatitudes, which are, without a doubt, the true picture of Jesus. In the Beatitudes, Jesus shows us what he is like. He reveals his nature, and he calls his listeners then and readers now *blessed*. For Dietrich Bonhoeffer, those who were present listening and who are reading his words today are blessed "because they have obeyed the call of Jesus, and the people as a whole because they are heirs of the promise...

But will they now claim their heritage by believing in Jesus Christ and his word?"[12] Being readers of the Word of God is one thing. Being doers of the Word is quite another. And the Beatitudes are a great place to start practicing living out God's Word.

A word of caution, though. Jesus does not give these Beatitudes as exhortations, saying this is how you should live. Instead, he's describing the condition of those who already truly follow God and what they will receive from him for their submission to him. There is no works-righteousness here. It is the Spirit of God who transforms us and empowers us to become who we should be so we can live as we should and find joy in life here as we anticipate the incredible life to come (Galatians 5). We cannot earn this life in any way. It is God's gift to us as he bestows his superabounding grace. All beatitude is from him. Our role is to trust him, yield to him, and cooperate with him. He does the rest.

Furthermore, Stanley Hauerwas and William H. Willimon observe that the Beatitudes tell us what God *has done* before any instruction is given about what we are to do. They write:

> Imagine a sermon that begins: "Blessed
> are you poor. Blessed are those of you
> who are hungry. Blessed are those of you
> who are unemployed. Blessed are those
> going through marital separation. Blessed
> are those who are terminally ill." The
> congregation does a double take.[13]

And, finally, when you take the Beatitudes in the context of the book of Matthew and its controlling theme of the kingdom of God, they become the banner of the entirety of Jesus' ministry.

- *Reread Matthew 5:1–12, and as you read through those verses, complete the following chart, noting the condition/trait and the result expressed in each of the Beatitudes (the first one has been completed for you):*

Verse	Condition/Trait	Result
3	*Spiritual poverty*	*The realm of the kingdom of heaven*
4		
5		
6		
7		
8		
9		
10		
11–12		

The Beatitudes list several traits of Christian character, and they close with Beatitudes wrapped around the world's reaction to living out those traits. They are interrelated and form a progression that when followed will certainly set a Christian apart from those who have yet to experience the true heart of Jesus. Let's take a closer look into each Beatitude, for they are meant to show us the way to "great happiness, prosperity, abundant goodness, and delight."[14]

Spiritual Poverty

The way to happiness begins with poverty of spirit (5:3). In 7:13, Jesus encourages entrance through the narrow gate. And this is certainly a way that will not be admired by the world, yet it is the foundation upon which God builds. Why? God cannot build unless pride, ambition, and the like are absent. Jeremiah 1:10 says, "See, I have set you this day over nations and over kingdoms, to pluck up and to break down, to destroy and to overthrow, to build and to plant" (ESV). When you embrace humility and surrender and a willingness to bow to God's sovereign control, you begin to approach spiritual poverty. For Jesus, that is the way to happiness: a life laid down and a life submitted to God.

- *God would love to see you empty so that he can see you filled and truly blessed. In Luke 16:14–17, Jesus calls out some religious leaders, addressing the issue of looking spiritual on the outside but not having a right heart on the inside. What are some areas in your life, as you reflect upon Matthew 5:3 and Luke 16:14–17, that you can lay down in favor of giving up control to God? Pride? Ambition? Stubbornness? Greed? Lust? List a few things that are the opposite of humility if you cannot come up with something. And remember, God's desire is to see his sons and daughters emptied of everything that prevents them from being humble in spirit.*

Waiting on the Lord

In Matthew 5:4, Jesus makes a guarantee. If you wait on the Lord, you will find what you are looking for. That sounds so amazing, right? You will be comforted. But it may take some time. In the Hebrew, the word *wait* also means "mourn or grieve." Mourning and grieving is a process, and God's timing is not always our timing. Psalm 31:15 says, "My life, my every moment, my destiny—it's all in your hands." Our time is in God's hands.

- *Have you ever mourned or grieved for the loss of a loved one? What was that process like? Maybe you're still grieving the loss of a loved one from many years ago. How did you find comfort in God? Was there a particular passage from Scripture that helped comfort you?*

- *Is there anything now that you're waiting on from the Lord? An answered prayer, perhaps? What is it?*

- *Overall, what has been your experience waiting on God? How has he responded to you?*

- *What have you learned and gained from the waiting? As the popular Christian song "Take Courage" notes, "He's in the waiting...He's never failing."*[15]

Gentleness

When you're gentle, you're much more likely to be content (Matthew 5:5). How does that work? Well, consider that gentleness can also be translated as meekness. Jesus is stating that a posture of quiet submission to God is the goal, and the result of that submission will be the earth as inheritance (Revelation 21–22). We can be content with what we have. We don't need to scrap and scramble for more. Instead, we need to rest in God, submitting to him and his ways. One day, that gentle spirit will be rewarded with everlasting life in the new heavens and new earth.

- *Turn to Revelation 21–22 and jot down what you learn about your future home.*

- *Is it worth waiting for? Does knowing what's to come make it easier to yield to God in the here and now, to be gentle in spirit? Why or why not?*

Craving Righteousness

There are a lot of things that can seemingly fulfill cravings: food, money, relationships, and even social status. Often, as humans, our life is spent in the pursuit of happiness, but that pursuit will undoubtedly end up in unfulfillment. Rather, Jesus names the pursuit of righteousness as the means to fruitfulness, which is a truer, more lasting sense of satisfaction (Matthew 5:6).

- *What does being righteous mean to you?*

- *How does righteousness relate to goodness and justice?*

- *What does a life in the pursuit of God's righteousness look like?*

Tender Mercy

One of the many characteristics of God is mercy. God shows compassion when the obvious result should be punishment. Jesus says as much in Luke 6:36: "Overflow with mercy and compassion for others, just as your heavenly Father overflows with mercy and compassion for all." When we show mercy to others, it's a direct result of our own experience in realizing that God has shown us a tremendous amount of mercy. Moreover, in Romans 5:8, Paul writes that "Christ proved God's passionate love for us by dying in our place while we were still lost and ungodly!" That is true mercy.

- *When we show mercy, it's a direct result of our own experience, realizing that God has shown us a tremendous amount of mercy. Have you experienced mercy in your life? Forgiveness from a family member or friend when it wasn't deserved? A second chance after making a mistake at work? How does experiencing mercy make it easier to show mercy?*

- *What did Jesus say we would experience if we showed mercy to others (Matthew 5:7)? Has this been what you have experienced? If not, why do you think you didn't?*

- *Micah 6:8 reminds us that the Lord requires us "to do justice, and to love kindness, and to walk humbly with [our] God" (ESV). Who are some examples of Christians who, through acts of mercy, have impacted the world around them?*

A Pure Heart

Jesus praised the pure of heart (Matthew 5:8), and yet the apostle Paul proclaimed that no one is pure—that is, completely free of evil: "The Scriptures agree, for it is written: There is no one who always does what is right, no, not even one!" (Romans 3:10). The promise of Jesus for the pure in heart, however, is that they will progressively see God. As we seek a heart that is more and more pure, we will experience more and more of God. And that is the ultimate goal of our journey: to see God! So while we still live with tainted hearts, the more we live for God, the more purified we become.

- *Think about someone you know who shows signs of a growing purity of heart. Perhaps the kindness of a grandparent comes to mind or maybe an expression of unconditional love from a family member or friend. What characteristics does this person demonstrate? How does his or her purity of heart reveal itself?*

- *How can you better guard your heart in your daily life so that the pursuit of a pure heart becomes more attainable?*

Making Peace

In John 14:27, Jesus says, "I leave the gift of peace with you—my peace. Not the kind of fragile peace given by the world, but my perfect peace." Through Jesus, we have access to a kind of peace that the world cannot provide—and not just the kind of peace that results in the lack of conflict. Through Jesus, we have access to peace that brings flourishing and wholeness.

- *Are you a peacemaker, or do you know someone who is? What are the characteristics you notice in a peacemaker?*

- *How can you improve at making peace in your life? Is there a relationship in your life that needs to improve? What steps can you take to make peace in that relationship?*

Persecution

No one wants to suffer. In fact, we spend a lot of our life attempting to make it as comfortable as possible. But Jesus calls us to be salt and light and to not hide our light. Read Matthew 5:10–16.

- *If we stand up for our faith, is persecution inevitable? Why or why not?*

- *Have you ever been persecuted for your belief in God? If so, how did that make you feel? If you haven't been persecuted, reflect on the reasons why.*

♥ SHARE GOD'S HEART

- *Do you regularly share your faith with others? If so, what does that look like? If not, why not?*

- *How can you work to better "light up the world" (5:14)?*

♥ EXPERIENCE GOD'S HEART

Have you heard the phrase "the struggle is real"? It was made popular online, and you've likely come across it in the form of a meme (a photograph with an amusing text written on it). But God certainly doesn't want us to struggle in our pursuit of living a life that reflects the Beatitudes.

- *Look back to the chart you filled out above. Which two or three Beatitudes caught your attention the most? List them below and write down an example of: (1) When you struggled to maintain the characteristic Jesus describes and (2) when you found success sustaining the characteristic over a period of time. As well, reflect upon the result of trying to live the particular Beatitudes you wrote about. When you succeeded in maintaining them, how did you experience the result? When you struggled, what was the result, and what did you find lacking in your life?*

- *Do you still struggle in any of these areas? Share your struggle with a trusted friend.*

Talking It Out

1. Choose one of the Beatitudes that you want to make a particular focus in your life over the next one or two weeks. Set a goal for how you plan to accomplish focusing on that particular Beatitude. Do you want to be gentler in your thoughts, words, and deeds (v. 5)? Then you may need an accountability partner, perhaps your spouse or someone from your small group. Maybe your focus will be seeking peace (v. 9), so you'll make it a goal to leave only positive, encouraging comments on social media posts, and you may want a friend to check your social media pages throughout the next few weeks.

2. In light of what you did in exercise one above, share with someone what results you experienced. Which results were expected, and which ones surprised you?

3. What did you learn through this application process?

4. Think back to what Jesus talks about in Matthew 5:10–11. It's almost as if he expects his followers to suffer and be persecuted. Do you know anyone who has no fear about approaching others to talk about Jesus? Talk with that individual about his or her boldness. Are you afraid to share Jesus with others because of the negativity you might experience? How can you overcome those fears? Ask that individual about some of his or her experiences, both good and bad. How can you be better prepared to preach the good news of Jesus and to "shine brightly before others" (v. 16)?

LESSON 4

The Sermon on the Hillside

Fulfilling the Law

(Matthew 5:17–6:33)

Jesus' accusers often brought up the argument that he was breaking the law. He healed a man with a shriveled hand on the Sabbath (Mark 3:1–6), and, on another occasion, he and his disciples picked grain to eat on the Sabbath (2:23–28), just to name a few instances. But Jesus had a different kind of response for them, stating that he did not come to set aside the law of Moses. Indeed, Jesus came as the culmination of the law: "If you think I've come to set aside the law of Moses or the writings of the prophets, you're mistaken. I have come to bring to perfection all that has been written" (Matthew 5:17). And while Jesus set a very high standard for Christian living in Matthew chapters 5 and 6, he knew that no one could live up to his standards. So what is Jesus looking for from his followers?

 **THE EXTRA MILE**

- *Did Jesus actually break the law of Moses, as the religious leaders of his day contended? If so, how could he break the law and yet remain sinless?*

- *When Jesus was confronted by the Pharisees in Matthew 12:9–13 for healing a man with a paralyzed hand, what was his response? Write your answer below:*

Given Jesus' response, it's a fair conclusion to say that he was confronting the religious hypocrisy of his day. Biblical commentator Matthew Henry puts it this way:

The Jewish teachers had corrupted many of
the commandments, by interpreting them
more loosely than they were intended;
a mistake which Christ discovered and
rectified (ch. 5) in his sermon on the mount:
but concerning the fourth commandment,
they had erred in the other extreme,
and interpreted it too strictly. Note, it is
common for men of corrupt minds, by their
zeal in rituals, and the external services of
religion, to think to atone for the looseness
of their morals.[16]

- *It's an age-old question, really. Would you steal food if
  you were hungry and had no other options? Stealing is
  breaking the law, but does that make it wrong? And while
  that example might be taking the concept to the extreme,
  Jesus definitely challenged religious tradition. What the
  religious teachers failed to understand, however, is that
  mercy is necessary at all times, especially on the Sabbath.
  How does mercy relate to the law, whether the law in
  Jesus' day or the law today?*

Did Jesus demand perfection? No! Why? Perfectionism is a
crushing weight. On the other hand, the pursuit of excellence, also
known as sanctification, is a life-long quest that results in greater
joy because of the vast amount of grace involved. Take a few minutes and read the article "Lay Aside the Weight of Perfection."[17]

- *After reading the article, answer these questions:*

  How did Jesus perfectly fulfill God's demand on us for perfection?

  How can you live a life free from perfectionism?

Hard Truths

Jesus hits his audience with some hard truths toward the end of Matthew 5, and he continues on into Matthew 6. Here's a quick list of a few that he mentions: anger equates to murder, a lustful look is tantamount to adultery, making oaths springs from the deceiver, don't repay an evil with evil, love your enemy, give in secret, fast privately, and avoid the trap of storing up treasures on the earth.

- *Read through Matthew 5:21–6:24. Which of the principles that Jesus teaches are the most difficult for you to internalize?*

- *Are you comfortable with being assessed as a murderer when you lash out in anger? Why?*

- *Have you ever bragged about your giving or fasting, or have you prayed extra loud to stand out in front of a group? Consider what Jesus says about this. What do you think about your actions now?*

💗 EXPERIENCE GOD'S HEART

God longs to be in communication with us. Look all the way back to the garden of Eden. In Genesis 3:8, God is described as "walking in the garden in the cool of the day" (ESV). God longs for us to be with him. And while we can't walk with him in Eden, we can pray.

- *Read Matthew 6:5–15. Prayer is not a duty. Rather, it is communication with God, talking with and listening to our Father in heaven. It's something we should do daily. Do you pray daily? Why or why not?*

- *According to verses 5–8, what should prayer look like? What shouldn't prayer look like?*

💙 SHARE GOD'S HEART

In Matthew 6:14–15, Jesus cautions against withholding forgiveness. An unforgiving heart is dangerous. It can lead to bitterness and a whole host of other issues. Hebrews 12:15 states: "Watch over each other to make sure that no one misses the revelation of God's grace. And make sure no one lives with a root of bitterness sprouting within them which will only cause trouble and poison the hearts of many."

- *Is there someone in your life whom you need to forgive? How have you dealt with the pain that he or she has caused you? Has your inability to forgive this person caused additional pain in your life?*

- *Spend time in prayer about your need to forgive this person. Ask God to change your heart toward this person so you can forgive him or her and move on in your life.*

Talking It Out

1. In Matthew 6:9–13, Jesus teaches us how to pray. It's a prayer that has become known as the Lord's Prayer. According to Bill Johnson and Mike Seth, Jesus used this prayer to teach two really important things: "First, when you worship God, you will become close to him. Second, prayer brings heaven to earth. When that happens, God's kingdom comes and helps people."[18] Given that statement, what do you see as the purpose of the Lord's Prayer?

2. There are six parts to the Lord's prayer. Pray through each part with a prayer partner and expand upon each section as you pray. What is being revealed in your heart as you pray?

- *Our Beloved Father, dwelling in the heavenly realms... (v. 9)*

- *Manifest your kingdom realm... (v. 10)*

- *We acknowledge you as our Provider... (v. 11)*

- *Forgive us the wrongs we have done... (v. 12)*

- *Rescue us... (v. 13)*

- *For you are the King who rules... (v. 13)*

3. In 6:31, Jesus calls on us to forsake our worries. Do you worry? Do you have any anxieties in life? Are you concerned about work, school, your family? Talk through your concerns with your spouse or with a friend. And remember what Jesus says about the birds: "Consider the birds—do you think they worry about their existence? They don't plant or reap or store up food, yet your heavenly Father provides them each with food. Aren't you much more valuable to your Father than they?" (v. 26).

LESSON 5

The Sermon on the Hillside

Reaping What You Sow

(Matthew 7)

The final part of the Sermon on the Hillside centers around Matthew 7:1–12 and what Jesus has to say about how we interact with others. "You reap what you sow" is a popular phrase, even in today's culture, and it's based upon Galatians 6:7–8.

> God will never be mocked! For what you
> plant will always be the very thing you
> harvest. The harvest you reap reveals
> the seed that you planted. If you plant
> the corrupt seeds of self-life into this
> natural realm, you can expect a harvest of
> corruption. If you plant the good seeds of
> Spirit-life you will reap beautiful fruits that
> grow from the everlasting life of the Spirit.

The writer of Galatians 6 definitely had this part of Jesus' sermon in mind where our Lord talks about judging others and the famed "Golden Rule." In God's natural order, reaping what we sow makes sense. New Testament scholar Jonathan T. Pennington notes: "One must choose how to live in relation to others, and this will affect one's experience of others and even God. If one has a condemning attitude toward others, this will be one's experience of the world; if one has a welcoming and accepting attitude, this will be one's experience."[19]

- *Read through Matthew 7:1–5 and then answer the questions that follow.*

    What faults do you tend to notice in others?

    What faults do others tend to notice in you?

    What was Jesus' warning for those who point out only the wrongs of others?

    What does Jesus call those who fail to acknowledge their own "blind spots"?

Judging others is a slippery slope. Think about a time when you made a flash judgment about someone close to you. How did it affect your relationship? What would have been a better way to handle the situation?

SHARE GOD'S HEART

Reread Matthew 7:6 as well as the corresponding study note. Wisdom can only be appreciated if you're willing to hear it.

- *How open are you to giving correction without condemnation? Likewise, how open are you to receiving correction? Rate yourself on a scale of 1–10. Why did you give yourself that rating?*

Revelation 22:14–15 says: "Wonderfully blessed are those who wash their robes white so they can access the Tree of Life and enter the city of bliss by its open gates. Those not permitted to enter are outside: the malicious hypocrites, the sexually immoral, sorcerers, murderers, idolaters, and every lover of lies."

- *It is our duty—with all the love and grace that we have been shown by our heavenly Father—to confront our fellow Christians caught up in sin. But first we have to deal with our own sin. Do you know someone who has a struggle similar to one you are going through? Maybe it's anger or a serious addiction. How can you work together to help each other?*

Ask, Seek, Knock

Jesus implores us to ask, seek, and knock in Matthew 7:7–8, and he takes it a step further, promising that when we ask, we will receive; when we seek, we will discover; and when we knock, the door will be opened for us. For minister D. Martyn Lloyd-Jones, "There is nothing that can be more encouraging as we face life with all its uncertainties and possibilities…This is the essence of the biblical message from beginning to end, this is the promise that comes to us."[20]

- *What have you recently asked God for?*

- *Did you get what you wanted? If you did, did the answer come when you expected it? If you're still waiting for your answer, how do you feel?*

🫶 EXPERIENCE GOD'S HEART

"The Golden Rule" found in Matthew 7:12 expands a bit upon the popular "do unto others as you want done to you" adage. For Jesus, it is "the essence of all the teachings of the Law and the prophets."

- *How does treating others like you want to be treated reflect the heart of God, even in the law revealed to Moses?*

- *Record a time when you were treated as you wanted to be. What did that communicate to you? How did you feel?*

- *Now record a time when you were not treated as you wanted to be. How did you feel? What did that communicate to you?*

The Way to Eternal Life

Jesus calls on us in verses 13–14 to follow a difficult path, and he explains that the "narrow gate" and the "difficult way" lead to eternal life.

- *What did Jesus mean when he said the narrow gate and the difficult way lead to eternal life and that few are able to find it?*

- *Why can the Christian life be so difficult but also so rewarding?*

DIGGING DEEPER

Starting in Matthew 7:15, Jesus gives warnings about false prophets and pretenders. In verse 16, he points to the ways in which they can be identified: "You can spot them by their actions, for the fruits of their character will be obvious. You won't find sweet grapes hanging on a thorn bush, and you'll never pick good fruit from a tumbleweed."

Second Peter 2:1–3 provides some additional insight into identifying false teachers:

> In the past there arose false prophets
> among God's people, just as there will
> continue to be false teachers who will
> secretly infiltrate in your midst to divide
> you, bringing with them their destructive
> heresies. They will even deny the Master,
> who paid the price for them, bringing
> swift destruction on themselves. Many
> will follow immoral lifestyles. Because
> of these corrupt false teachers, the way
> of truth will be slandered. They are only
> out for themselves, ready to exploit you
> for their own gain through their cunning
> arguments. Their condemnation has been
> a long time coming. But their destruction
> does not slumber or sit idly by, for it is sure
> to come.

Compare that with how true believers are described in 2 Peter 1:5–7:

> So devote yourselves to lavishly
> supplementing your faith with goodness,
> and to goodness add understanding, and
> to understanding add the strength of self-

control, and to self-control add patient endurance, and to patient endurance add godliness, and to godliness add mercy toward your brothers and sisters, and to mercy toward others add unending love.

There are several means by which to recognize false teachers. Some false teachers will make up stories and not follow sound doctrine. Some will avoid preaching messages centered on Christ. Some will live immoral lives. And some will just flat out be the opposite of the characteristics of a true believer listed above.

- *Have you ever been exposed to false teachings or a false teacher? What did you do?*

- *What options did you have for confronting the false teachers with whom you've had experience?*

- *Perhaps you have family members or friends who follow false teachers or teachings. What can you do to help them see the errors that have a grip on them?*

Talking It Out

1. What does Jesus mean when he says, "The measurement you use on them will be used on you" (Matthew 7:2)? Why does Jesus seem so stern here? Why is it so important, as a Christian, not to be judgmental and hypocritical?

2. How does Psalm 51:16–17 relate to what Jesus says in the opening verses of Matthew 7?

3. Why is humility so important? And how was Jesus the ultimate example of humility?

4. Discuss some ways you can help cultivate humility in your life.

LESSON 6

Power

(Matthew 8–10)

Philip Yancey observes, "A sign is not the same thing as proof; a sign is merely a marker for someone who is looking in the right direction."[21] Certainly, there were many signs pointing to the fact that Jesus was the promised Messiah, the Christ. That he was indeed the Son of God. But the many miracles that are recorded in the Gospels are the proof. And according to John, Jesus offered a lot of proof: "Jesus did countless things that I haven't included here. And if every one of his works were written down and described one by one, I suppose that the world itself wouldn't have enough room to contain the books that would have to be written!" (John 21:25).

Jesus performed miracles for several reasons. First, he was compassionate. Mark writes: "Being deeply moved with tender compassion, Jesus reached out and touched the skin of the leper and told him, 'Of course I want you to be healed—so now, be cleansed!'" (Mark 1:41). Second, Jesus' miracles proved he was who he said he was, the Son of God. Acts 2:22 reinforces this idea; Jesus' miracles substantiated his claims: "Jesus, the Victorious, was a man on a divine mission whose authority was clearly proven. For you know how God performed many powerful miracles, signs, and wonders through him." Finally, Jesus' miracles demonstrate that we have access to a new spiritual reality, the kingdom of God.

Jesus' Miraculous Power

Jesus demonstrated power with four types of miracles that Matthew records in chapters 8 and 9: (1) power over sickness; (2) power over the forces of nature; (3) power over demons; and (4) power over death. For each miracle listed below, read the accompanying verses, assign to the miracle one of the four types of power, and write a two or three sentence description of the importance of the miracle.

- *Jesus heals a leper (Matthew 8:1–4)*

    Type of power:

    Description of the miracle's importance:

- *Jesus heals the son of a Roman officer (vv. 5–13)*

    Type of power:

    Description of the miracle's importance:

- *Jesus heals Peter's mother-in-law (vv. 14–15)*

    Type of power:

    Description of the miracle's importance:

- *Jesus calms a storm (vv. 23–27)*

    Type of power:

    Description of the miracle's importance:

- *Jesus sets free two demonized men (vv. 28–33)*

    Type of power:

    Description of the miracle's importance:

- *Jesus heals a paralyzed man (9:2–8)*

    Type of power:

    Description of the miracle's importance:

- *Jesus heals Jairus' daughter (vv. 18–19, 23–26)*

    Type of power:

    Description of the miracle's importance:

- *Jesus heals a woman suffering from continual bleeding (vv. 20–22)*

    Type of power:

    Description of the miracle's importance:

- *Jesus heals two blind men (vv. 27–29)*

    Type of power:

    Description of the miracle's importance:

- *Jesus heals a demonized, mute man (vv. 32–33)*

    Type of power:

    Description of the miracle's importance:

 # EXPERIENCE GOD'S HEART

In Matthew 10:1–15, Jesus officially commissions his closest followers, the twelve apostles. He specifically "imparted to them authority to cast out demons and to heal every sickness and every disease" (v. 1). In other words, Jesus let his followers know that they have the ability to perform miracles, just like him. There are numerous accounts of Jesus' followers demonstrating the same power that he used and imparted to them. For example, read Mark 6:7–13 and Luke 9:1–6.

- *With what mission did Jesus charge his followers? What power did his followers demonstrate?*

- *Jesus' twelve apostles were seemingly common men, men who weren't famous or important leaders when they began following him. Like them, you may be an ordinary Christian, a simple follower of Jesus who goes about his or her daily life, working, raising a family, etc. Still, you have access to the same power that Jesus imparted to his disciples. In fact, Jesus said his followers will walk in even greater power than he did: "I tell you this timeless truth: The person who follows me in faith, believing in me, will do the same mighty miracles that I do—even greater miracles than these because I go to be with my Father!" (John 14:12). Are you walking in that power? Why or why not? How could you be encouraged to have the faith required to walk in such power?*

♥ SHARE GOD'S HEART

- *Have you witnessed the miraculous power of Jesus in your own life? Provide an example or two.*

- *Have you prayed for healing in others? If yes, write down a few thoughts about the experience. If not, why not? Pray and ask God for the faith to be bold and pray for healing in others.*

Talking It Out

1. Jesus commanded the twelve apostles to "continually bring healing to lepers and to those who are sick, and make it your habit to break off the demonic presence from people, and raise the dead back to life" (Matthew 10:8). Why is such power necessary when telling others about Jesus?

2. What happens if you pray for healing for someone and they don't get healed? Bill Johnson relates the following: "The mandate on every believer is to do as Jesus did; we have been given a commission to heal the sick, raise the dead and cast out demons (see Matt 10:8). He started something that we are to complete. Having received His Holy Spirit, we now have the great privilege of walking in the same anointing Jesus Himself walked in. Jesus already decided to heal and paid the ultimate price for our healing and freedom with His life. If we pray for someone and they don't get healed, that doesn't change our assignment. God is looking to co-labor with us to fulfill His purpose on earth to establish His Kingdom and reveal His goodness."[22] Does Johnson's encouragement to not give up in the face of a seemingly unanswered prayer for healing encourage you to continue praying for the sick? Why or why not?

LESSON 7

Unexpected Messiah, Lord of the Sabbath

(Matthew 11–12)

Jesus was not the promised Messiah that the Jewish people expected. It's probably fair to say that the only person who expected Jesus to be the kind of Messiah that he was, was Jesus himself. After all, even his closest followers went into hiding after his death (John 20:20–23). Bible scholar N. T. Wright explains it this way:

> There were, to be sure, ways of coping with the death of a teacher, or even a leader...The category of failed but still revered Messiah, however, did not exist. A Messiah who died at the hands of the pagans, instead of winning [God's] battle against them, was a deceiver...Why then did people go on talking about Jesus of Nazareth, except as a remarkable but tragic memory? The obvious answer is that... Jesus was raised from the dead.[23]

Most Jews expected a conquering Messiah—one who would liberate them from their gentile oppressors. But, as the apostle

Paul writes, Jesus was quite different: "He emptied himself of his outward glory by reducing himself to the form of a lowly servant. He became human! He humbled himself and became vulnerable, choosing to be revealed as a man and was obedient. He was a perfect example, even in his death—a criminal's death by crucifixion!" (Philippians 2:7–8). Jesus was the unexpected Messiah, and as such, he accomplished far more for far more people than he would have as a military leader and conqueror.[24]

Jesus and John

One way Jesus set himself apart from other messengers from God was the comparison and contrast he made between himself and John the Baptizer. By doing this, he further established how he, as the prophesied Christ, was greater than those who came before him.

- *Read Matthew 11:1–15. In the following chart, write down on the right-hand side what Jesus said about himself and on the left-hand side what he said about John.*

John the Baptizer	Jesus the Christ

- *In Matthew 11:4–6, Jesus tells John's disciples to report back to him that the Scriptures are being fulfilled: the blind can see and the deaf can hear (Isaiah 29:18); the paralyzed can walk and the mute can talk (35:6); and broken hearts are healed (61:1). Why was it important for Jesus to offer proof that he was fulfilling Old Testament prophesies?*

- *What did Jesus mean when he said, "I tell you the truth, throughout history there has never been a man who surpasses John the Baptizer. Yet the least of those who now experience heaven's kingdom will become even greater than he. From the moment John stepped onto the scene until now, the realm of heaven's kingdom is bursting forth, and passionate people have taken hold of its power" (Matthew 11:11–12). Hint: Read Micah 2, especially verses 12–13. How did John prepare hearts for the arrival of Jesus?*

Jesus and His Generation

- *After Jesus compared himself to John, he talked to the crowd (Matthew 11:7) about the generation to whom he was ministering (vv. 16–19). What does he say about them, including how they responded to John as well as to him, the Son of Man?*

- *What role does God's wisdom play in Jesus' assessment (v. 19)?*

Jesus versus Unbelieving Cities

Still speaking to the crowd, Jesus denounced various cities for their negative response to him.

- *Which cities did he criticize, and what were his charges against them (vv. 20–24)?*

- *What did Jesus say would be the end of such cities?*

Jesus and the Heavenly Father

Jesus also spoke to the heavenly Father so the crowd could hear him.

- *What did Jesus say about the Father (vv. 25–27)?*

- *What did Jesus say about his relationship with the Father (v. 27)?*

🧡 EXPERIENCE GOD'S HEART

Jesus closes his time with the crowd with a welcoming invitation (vv. 28–30).

- *Whom did Jesus single out (v. 28)?*

- *What did he say he would offer them, and what would they need to do to receive his offer (vv. 28–30)?*

- *Consider some of the things Jesus endured in Matthew 11: the imprisonment of John (v. 2) and the failure of the people to turn their lives fully over to God despite Jesus' miraculous work (vv. 20–23). What was Jesus' response (v. 27)?*

- *In what ways are you experiencing setbacks in your life? How do the truths that Jesus knew provide you with comfort?*

❤ SHARE GOD'S HEART

- *Do you have family or friends who are experiencing any heavy burdens? How can you help comfort them? And to whom can you point to help them find rest and refreshment?*

Jesus and the Sabbath

Perhaps one of the most challenging aspects of Jesus' ministry, which made his claims to be the Messiah difficult to accept—at least to the religious leaders of his day—was how he tended to break with religious tradition. This was especially the case when Jesus, by his deeds and teaching, violated Jewish traditions concerning the Sabbath.

- *Read Matthew 12:1–21 and then answer the questions that follow:*

  What did Jesus do that evoked such a strong reaction from the Pharisees?

Who were witnesses of what Jesus did and said?

What was Jesus' defense of his actions on the Sabbath?

How did the Pharisees respond to him?

How did the crowds respond to him?

What was Jesus' response, first to his critics and then to the crowds?

🄝 WORD WEALTH

Jesus did not break any laws (refer back to Lesson 4). But he definitely challenged the way that the law was interpreted by the religious leaders of his day. Jesus says in Matthew 12:8 that he has "lordship over the Sabbath." The Greek word for *lordship* that Jesus uses here is *kurios*, meaning "supreme in authority." It literally means that Jesus had all the power and all the authority. He could do whatever he desired. Instead, however, he offers a correction: "The Sabbath was made for the sake of people, and not people for the Sabbath" (Mark 2:27).

- *What does Jesus mean that the Sabbath was made for the people? What do you think was God's point in establishing a day of rest?*

Jesus goes on to provide evidence that the entire point of the Sabbath has been missed: (1) At one point, King David and his men ate bread that was lawfully reserved for the priests; (2) No one would fail to rescue a fallen lamb just because it was the Sabbath. It's important to note here that Jesus' challenge has nothing to do with the importance of rest (as God commanded in the fourth commandment; see Exodus 20:8). Rather, it has everything to do with the one who is the Lord of the Sabbath. Dr. Ligon Duncan offers this sage advice:

And, you see, that's the real key to your Lord's Day. You want to enjoy the Lord's Day? The only way to enjoy the Lord's Day is to enjoy the Lord of the Lord's Day. That's the whole key to enjoying the Lord's Day. If you don't enjoy the lord of the Lord's Day, the Lord's Day is going to be miserable![25]

- *What is the significance in Jesus, despite having "supreme authority" over the Sabbath, not abolishing the Sabbath and, instead, shifting its focus?*

- *Do you observe the Sabbath? Do you "enjoy the Lord's Day"? Why or why not?*

- *Read Matthew 11:28–30. What is it like to have true rest in Jesus?*

- *Do you believe God is more concerned with strict adherence to a day of rest or that we best practice rest in our daily lives? Provide evidence from Matthew 12 to support your answer.*

 THE EXTRA MILE

Why did Jesus offer up evidence to support his actions? Quite simply, he's making a point of intent of law. *Intent of law* is a modern legal term that has to do with the reason a violation of law is committed. Some individuals may choose not to follow a certain law due to their immediate circumstances and needs. Read the account of King David and his men eating the holy bread that was only to be consumed by the priests found in 1 Samuel 20:1–9.

- *Why were David and his men hungry? Why didn't they have access to food?*

- *How was David able to convince the priest to allow them to eat the bread?*

When David took a census against God's command in 1 Chronicles 21, Israel faced severe consequences in the form of a deadly pestilence that killed seventy thousand. Yet there was no punishment for David and his men for eating the holy bread.

- *Compare God's requirements for a census tax in Exodus 30:11–16 with God's command to leave food available in fields for the sake of hungry travelers in Deuteronomy 23:24–25. What were God's specific requirements for conducting a census? What do you think was the intent behind God's detailed rules for taking a census? How was David's intent different when he took a census versus when he ate the holy bread?*

- *How can strict adherence to Sabbath observance altogether miss the point of the Sabbath?*

Jesus versus Satan

The Pharisees provided a stunning explanation for Jesus' ability to cast out demons from people who were possessed. Their explanation was actually meant as an indictment to move people away from concluding that Jesus might be the long-awaited Messiah. This event launched Jesus' defense of his actions and his own indictment of those who chose to work against him.

- *What miracle did Jesus perform that amazed the crowd and led them to wonder if he was the Messiah (Matthew 12:22–23)?*

- *What explanation of Jesus' miracle-working power did the Pharisees offer (v. 24)?*

- *What argument did Jesus offer to counter the Pharisees' indictment (vv. 25–29)?*

- *In light of Jesus' argument, he draws two major conclusions:*

Summarize Jesus' first conclusion (v. 30).

Summarize his second conclusion (vv. 31–32).

 # DIGGING DEEPER

Jesus was a master logician. He knew how to reason well, and he used this ability "not to win battles, but to achieve understanding or insight in his hearers."[26] He didn't try to force assent; instead, he strove to persuade so as to change people from the inside. As Christian philosopher Dallas Willard explains, Jesus "typically aims at real inward change of view that would enable his hearers to become significantly different as people through the workings of their own intellect. They will have, unless they are strongly resistant to the point of blindness, the famous 'eureka' experience, not the experience of being outdone or beaten down."[27]

In Matthew 12:25–29, Jesus uses his ability to reason to counter the Pharisees' claim that he performed miracles by the power of Satan. First, Jesus makes a statement that anyone should accept: "Any kingdom that fights against itself is reduced to ruins. And any family or community splintered by strife will fall apart" (v. 25). In other words, a house divided will not stand. From here, Jesus takes the position of the Pharisees and reduces it to absurdity. Given that a kingdom turned against itself cannot survive, how then can Satan sustain his own kingdom if he is "making war on himself" (v. 26)? The expected answer is that he cannot. Jesus then further reduces the Pharisees' claim to absurdity with a question: "If Satan empowers me to cast out demons, who empowers your exorcists to cast them out?" (v. 27). Based on what the Pharisees claimed about Jesus' ability to exorcise demons, logically they would have to apply their claim to other Jewish exorcists. Jesus' assumption is that they will not do this. What Jesus has done is to show the Pharisees that they have committed a logical fallacy called *reductio ad absurdum*, and he has done so flawlessly.[28]

Now he moves to the true source of his power, the Holy Spirit. Since Satan is not at war with himself, who is at war with him? God is! Says Jesus, "If I drive out demons by the power of the Spirit of God, then the end of Satan's kingdom has come!" (v. 28). The only being who can beat Satan is the Creator himself, and this he is doing through his Spirit who is working through his Son, Jesus. Jesus is, in effect, plundering Satan's house (v. 29).

Jesus and the Pharisees

Jesus wasn't finished dealing with the Pharisees, though he had refuted their false claim about the source of his power. First, he talks about the difference between good trees and rotten trees.

- *How can you tell if a tree is good (v. 33)?*

- *How can you tell if it is rotten (v. 33)?*

- *How does Jesus use his illustration about trees to identify the condition of the Pharisees and those who speak and act similarly (vv. 34–37)?*

- *In the long run, why do the differences between goodness and rottenness matter?*

The second matter Jesus deals with regarding the Pharisees (and some Jewish scholars who were with them) was their call on him to perform a miraculous sign for them (v. 38). Notice that they didn't acknowledge all the miracles of healing and exorcism Jesus had already performed. Instead, they wanted him to perform a miracle that would wow them!

- *What was Jesus' response to this call on him to perform a miracle at the Pharisees' demand (vv. 39–42)?*

Still addressing the Pharisees as well as those with them, Jesus returns to the subject of demon possession and links it with another warning.

- *What does Jesus say about how an exorcised person can end up in worse shape (vv. 43–45)?*

- *To whom does Jesus apply this warning (v. 45)?*

Jesus and Family

Matthew 12 ends with Jesus still speaking to the crowds, and this time the subject turns to family.

- *What prompts Jesus to speak about family (vv. 46–47)?*

- *Who does Jesus say is his true family and what makes them so (vv. 48–50)?*

Talking It Out

1. This lesson focuses quite a bit on the Sabbath and the law and Jesus' tendency to buck the system, so to speak, in favor of showing people God's true heart. Have you ever found yourself going to church on Sunday simply because it's just what you do? What are some ways that you can guard your heart so that religious duty doesn't take precedence over connecting with the heart of God?

2. What does Jesus mean when he says, "You have hidden the great revelation of your authority from those who are proud and think they are wise" (Matthew 11:25)? Compare 1 Corinthians 1:18–2:2. In what ways could you be considered too proud? How could you act with more humility? Read 1 Corinthians 1:27–28. In what ways could you better receive the truth found in God's Word?

3. For Jesus, family consists of those who follow him. He doesn't disown or put down his mother and brothers, but he shows us that his family goes beyond the bounds of biology (Matthew 12:46–50). Are you a member of God's forever family? How do you know? Do you see those who follow Jesus as your family? Why or why not?

LESSON 8

Parables of the Kingdom Realm

(Matthew 13)

Matthew, Mark, Luke, and John record Jesus telling over thirty parables. In particular, the Gospel of Matthew records seven of them in chapter 13. And these parables give great insight into the kingdom realm.

So how does Jesus describe the kingdom of God? Is it peaceful and prosperous? Is it a place of perfect health and excess wealth? Does Jesus provide a blueprint for the proper way by which to organize a government? Hardly! Rather, he reveals through his kingdom parables the ways by which we can find and participate in his kingdom realm.

The Parables

Review each parable from Matthew 13. Then write your own summary and what you believe is the meaning of each parable as it relates to the kingdom of God. Hint: If you need some help with the meanings, Jesus explains the meanings of some of the parables in verses 36–43. The study note for verse 44 is very helpful as well.

- *The parable of the seed (vv. 3–9)*

    Summary:

    Meaning:

- *The parable of the weeds (vv. 24–30)*

    Summary:

    Meaning:

- *The parable of the tiny mustard seed (vv. 31–32)*

   Summary:

   Meaning:

- *The parable of the yeast (v. 33)*

   Summary:

   Meaning:

- *The parable of the hidden treasure (v. 44)*

    Summary:

    Meaning:

- *The parable of an extraordinary pearl (vv. 45–46)*

    Summary:

    Meaning:

• *The parable of the fishing net (vv. 47–50)*

   Summary:

   Meaning:

 EXPERIENCE GOD'S HEART

Have you figured it out? Have you started to get a grasp on Jesus' kingdom realm and what the reality of living a kingdom realm life is like?

• *What are some practical ways in which we can respond to Jesus' invitation to enter into his kingdom realm?*

- *After Jesus taught the selection of parables recorded in Matthew 13, he returned to his hometown, Nazareth. At first people were astonished by the revelation they heard from him, but soon they "became offended and began to turn against him" (v. 57). Have the words of Jesus ever offended you? Reflect on any offense the words of Jesus may have caused you, including what that offense revealed about you and what you needed to learn. Record what you realized about yourself and your situation in the space provided.*

♥ SHARE GOD'S HEART

In verse 52, Jesus relates that those who understand the kingdom realm are like homeowners whose homes are filled many treasures (old and new). It's up to us to know what treasures to bring out and when to show them to others.

- *What are some of your favorite treasures that you've discovered in the kingdom realm? Maybe you've turned from sin, discovered a rich prayer life, or developed an insatiable thirst for reading the Bible. Record your answer here.*

- *When was the last time you shared a kingdom treasure with a friend? Write down some thoughts about your experience. If you cannot think of a time lately, maybe it's time. Write down a few names that come to mind and a few treasures you'd love to share with each of them.*

Talking It Out

1. To truly live a kingdom lifestyle, what should followers of Christ pursue? What shouldn't they go after?

2. In the parable of the fishing net, the net captures both good and bad fish. But in the end, only the good fish are collected into baskets. The kingdom of God is for everyone, good and bad. How do you justify sharing the gospel message and all the accompanying treasures of the kingdom realm with those who seemingly don't deserve it? Who brings the final judgment?

3. In Matthew 13:57, Jesus said, "There's only one place a prophet isn't honored—his own hometown!" Why do you think that's true? Why would those who were familiar with Jesus reject him, especially if they couldn't find fault with his teachings?

LESSON 9

The Son of God

(Matthew 14–17)

There's a lot going on in Matthew 14–17. John the Baptizer dies. Jesus performs numerous miracles, including feeding thousands of people and walking on water. Peter makes his famous confession about who he believes Jesus is. And there's Jesus' glorious transfiguration.

All these happenings point to one overarching theme: that Jesus is the Christ, the Son of God, which, in turn, highlights his relationship with the Father, his role as the Messiah, and his divine nature. Saddened by the death of John the Baptist, Jesus turned to God the Father. Confirmed by Peter as the Anointed One, Jesus prophesied both his death and resurrection. And when confronted with challenges, he met the needy with miraculous mercy.

📖 THE BACKSTORY

According to Matthew 14:1–2, when Herod heard about Jesus, he was certain that Jesus was actually John the Baptizer raised from the dead. Read 14:1–12. It's a very dramatic story. The wild prophet confronts the wicked ruler for marrying his own brother's wife. The evil ruler's evil wife hatches a scheme. And John's head ends up on a platter. It's also a very gruesome story. But why did Herod even care what John had to say?

Herod Antipas ruled from 4 BC to AD 39 over the Jewish provinces of Galilee and Perea, which were under Roman rule. He was the son of Herod the Great and was not the sole heir; therefore, Rome only assigned him partial rule over his father's kingdom.[29] In order to improve his position and earn Rome's trust, Herod Antipas sought to keep the lands he governed calm. So despite having some affinity for John (cf. Mark 6:20), he imprisoned him, certainly in response to his condemnation of Herod's marriage to Herodias and partially because he perceived that John presented a danger to the safety of his region. John was popular, after all, and gathered large crowds (see Luke 3, especially vv. 7, 10, and 15).

Compassion for the Multitude

- *What did Jesus do after hearing about John's execution (Matthew 14:12–14)?*

- *Along with healing the sick, how did Jesus meet the needs of the multitude (vv. 15–21)?*

- *Why did Jesus do these things for those who flocked around him (v. 14)?*

- *Have you ever sought to meet the needs of others even though you originally wanted to do something for yourself? Describe what you did and how it worked out for you and those you served.*

Revelation-Insight

- *What did Jesus do after the crowd had been fed (vv. 22–23)?*

- *Why do you think Jesus chose to be alone to pray after a full day of ministry?*

- *When do you typically choose to pray?*

- *What can you learn from Jesus' example about other times to pray?*

- *While Jesus was praying, what was going on with his disciples (v. 24)?*

- *How did Jesus reach his disciples, and what did they do in response to him (vv. 25–33)?*

Hypocritical Critics and Clueless Followers

Even as the news about Jesus and his amazing work and teaching continued to spread throughout the land (vv. 34–36), some of the most revered Jewish religious leaders came from Jerusalem, the religious center of Judaism, to question and criticize Jesus over his disciples' lack of adherence to the traditions about ceremonially washing their hands (15:1–2).

- *What was Jesus' counter charge to these religious leaders (vv. 3, 6–9)?*

- *What evidence did Jesus provide in support of his charge (vv. 4–6)?*

- *Jesus used his encounter as a teaching moment for the other people who were near him. What did he tell them and how did this further answer the religious leaders' emphasis on outward obedience to traditions (vv. 10–14)?*

- *Peter, as the usual spokesman for the other disciples, asked Jesus to explain his teaching (v. 15). Summarize Jesus' response (vv. 16–20).*

Honoring Faith

When Jesus entered a gentile region called Lebanon, a "Canaanite woman" sought him out (vv. 21–22). Matthew's mention that she was a Canaanite meant that she was not only a non-Jew, a pagan, but of the ancestry of the ancient enemies of God's covenant people. And yet in contrast to those leaders of the covenant people who found Jesus and his disciples offensive and challenged them so often, this woman—who had no claim on the God of the covenant and who even came from a people who stood against God's people—called Jesus "Lord, Son of David" (v. 22). She approached "the Jewish Messiah and with great faith [asked] only for grace."[30]

- *What did this woman ask of Jesus (v. 22)?*

- *How did Jesus initially respond to her and why (vv. 23–24)?*

- *Summarize the subsequent exchange between this woman and Jesus (vv. 25–27).*

- *Did this woman eventually receive what her faith and persistence desired (v. 28)?*

⦿ DIGGING DEEPER

Jesus' aphorism in verse 26 reflects the common Jewish attitude toward gentiles, seeing them as dogs, outside of God's covenant with Israel. New Testament scholar F. F. Bruce suggests that Jesus may have said this with "a twinkle in his eye," inviting the woman through his look and tone of voice to continue to persevere in making her request. In other words, his statement may have suggested to her, "'You know what we Jews are supposed to think of you Gentiles; do you think it is right for you to come and ask for a share in the healing which I have come to impart to Jews?'"[31] Whether or not this was the case, the woman, as Bible scholar D. A. Carson points out, remains "confident that even if she is not entitled to sit down as a guest at Messiah's table, Gentile 'dog' that she is, yet at least she may be allowed to receive a crumb of the uncovenanted mercies of God." And that she definitely received! In fact, when Jesus tells her that he will grant her request, he uses the Greek term "o," an exclamation that carries great "emotional force."[32]

Healing and Feeding

After Jesus left Lebanon, he traveled to a hill near Lake Galilee and ministered to the crowds who came to him (vv. 29–30).

- *How did Jesus help the crowds (v. 30)?*

• *How did they respond to what Jesus did (v. 31)?*

• *What else did Jesus do to serve those who came to him for help (vv. 32–38)?*

Demand for a Sign

In Matthew 16:1–4, the Sadducees demanded that Jesus prove he was the Messiah by producing a supernatural sign. It's important to note here that the Sadducees, as a religious group, denied the supernatural (see the study notes for 16:1).

• *What was Jesus' response to the Sadducees' demand?*

- *Why do you think this would have been an odd request by the Sadducees? What was the intent of their challenge?*

- *Have you ever demanded proof from God? Write down a few thoughts about your experience in making demands of God. Share those thoughts with a fellow believer.*

A Warning

After the miraculous feeding of the four thousand, the disciples lament that they had forgotten to bring any bread with them (v. 5). In response, Jesus uses the occasion not to talk about physical bread but to warn the disciples, "Watch out for the yeast of the Pharisees and the Sadducees" (v. 6). In Scripture, "yeast" is "a common symbol for evil...and could therefore be applied to different kinds of wickedness (e.g., Luke 12:1; cf. Exod 34:25; Lev 2:11; 1 Cor 5:6–8), but always with the idea that a little of it could have a far-reaching and insidious effect."[33] But the disciples found Jesus' comment confusing (Matthew 16:7–8), and this led to Jesus' rebuke.

- *Summarize what Jesus told his disciples (vv. 8–11).*

- *Did the disciples eventually grasp what Jesus was getting at (v. 12)?*

Carson points out that Jesus didn't always find the teachings of the Pharisees and Sadducees in error. He stood with the Sadducees against the Pharisees on the authority of Halakah (rules of conduct derived from interpretations of Scripture, preserved in oral tradition) and with the Pharisees against the Sadducees on the Resurrection (22:23–33). The "teaching of the Pharisees and Sadducees" to which Jesus refers ([16]:5–12), therefore, is an attitude of unbelief toward divine revelation that could not perceive Jesus to be the Messiah (vv. 1–4) but that tried to control and tame the Messiah they claimed to await. The disciples are to avoid that.[34]

- *Are there any teachings about Jesus that you used to believe but later learned were false? If so, what were they? How did you come to see that they were in error?*

Jesus' Identity and True Discipleship

With his closest followers sitting around him, Jesus engaged them in a pivotal teaching session about his identity and true discipleship.

- *Jesus drew out of his disciples what others were saying about him. What were these views (Matthew 16:13–14)?*

- *When Jesus asked them who they believed he was, what did Peter, their spokesman, say, and what did Jesus say about the source of Peter's knowledge (vv. 15–17)?*

- *Jesus then added instruction about the church and the authority it will have. After reading verses 18–19 and consulting the study notes on these verses, summarize in your own words Jesus' teaching here.*

- *Jesus once again explained to the disciples what lay in store for him in Jerusalem (v. 21). What was Peter's response (v. 22)? How did Jesus react to what Peter said (v. 23)?*

- *Jesus ends his teaching session by talking about the essence of becoming a true follower of him and some of the benefits that will come (vv. 24–28). As you read through this teaching, write down the essentials of a true disciple of Jesus, then add what benefits will be given to such followers.*

The Glorious Transfiguration

When Peter, James, and John witnessed Jesus' transfiguration in Matthew 17:1–13, they saw Jesus' appearance "dramatically altered": "sun poured from his face" and "his clothing became luminescent" (v. 2). Representing the law and the prophets respectively, Moses and Elijah appeared, and God spoke. As Jesus approached his death and resurrection, he underwent a change in form, and he revealed and proved yet again that he was, indeed, the Son of God and that the kingdom realm had arrived.

Read the study notes for Matthew 17:2 and read Romans 12:2 and 2 Corinthians 3:18.

- *Why was the transfiguration necessary? Remember, God had already spoken over Jesus when John baptized him, and Peter had already confessed that Jesus was the promised Messiah.*

- *How was Jesus' transformation into a glorified form a foreshadowing for Jesus and for us?*

DIGGING DEEPER

Even prior to witnessing the transfiguration, Peter testified to Jesus' true nature. Matthew records him as saying, "You are the Anointed One, the Son of the living God!" (Matthew 16:16). But what does it mean that Jesus was called the Son of God? John 3:17 and 11:27 describe Jesus as the preexistent Son of God. Indeed, Jesus was sent into the world by God the Father. Yet, everything was created through the Son, and nothing was created without him (John 1:3). So, his sonship is not the kind of biological father-son relationship we are used to on earth. Rather, Jesus' sonship exemplifies how a relationship with God the Father should look. His purpose, as the Son of God, was to do God's will and bring salvation to humankind. As the Son of God, Jesus exemplifies a perfect relationship with the Father.

- *As the Son of God, how did Jesus show what a relationship with God should be like?*

- *Read Psalm 2:7–9. King David was called a son. How was David a prophetic prototype of Jesus?*

 EXPERIENCE GOD'S HEART

Consider again 2 Corinthians 3:18:

> We can all draw close to him with the veil removed from our faces. And with no veil we all become like mirrors who brightly reflect the glory of the Lord *Jesus*. We are being transfigured into his very image as we move from one brighter level of glory to another. And this glorious transfiguration comes from the Lord, who is the Spirit.

- *What does it mean to be transformed (transfigured) into the image of Christ?*

- *Another translation says, "we...are progressively being transformed" (AMP). How is being transfigured into the image of Christ like sanctification (being set free from the power of sin)?*

- *As we are transformed and drawn ever closer to God, what are our responsibilities to him as his sons and daughters?*

❤ SHARE GOD'S HEART

When Jesus meets a man with a son who has epilepsy, the man reveals that his disciples were not able to heal him. Jesus responds, "Where is your faith?...How much longer do I stay with you and put up with your doubts?" (Matthew 17:17).

- *If confronted with a similar situation—that is, if someone comes to you for prayer or healing—will you crumble under the pressure? Will you be prepared? How is your faith level?*

- *What are some strategies you can use to shore up your faith?*

- *What does Jesus mean when he promises that you'll be able to move mountains if you have "faith inside of you no bigger than the size of a small mustard seed" (v. 20)?*

Tax Help

Even after Jesus had told his disciples earlier about his impending arrest, execution, and resurrection, and even after he had taught them more about faith and healing, when he reminded them of the events he would soon face, the disciples "were devastated" (vv. 22–23). The idea that Jesus would die grieved them, and they apparently still didn't comprehend his resurrection.

Sometime later, tax collectors asked Peter if Jesus paid the temple tax, to which Peter answered yes before ever talking to Jesus about it (vv. 24–25). Jesus, aware of what Peter had done, asked him: "Who pays tolls or taxes to a king? Is tax collected from the king's own children, or from his subjects" (v. 25).

• *What is Peter's answer to Jesus' question (v. 26)?*

• *How does Jesus respond to Peter (v. 27)?*

What is Jesus' point here? D. A. Carson explains: "The point is that, just as royal sons are exempt from the taxes imposed by their fathers, so too Jesus is exempt from the 'tax' imposed by his Father. In other words Jesus acknowledges the temple tax to be an obligation to God; but since he is uniquely God's Son, therefore he is exempt (v. 26)…Exempt though he is, Jesus will pay the tax so as not to offend."[35] So he miraculously covers the tax for himself and for Peter.

Talking It Out

1. Do you understand the difference Jesus makes between outward compliance (15:17–20) and the reality within? Why do you think this difference matters? Can you provide examples of people who adhere to outward "virtue" while apparently ignoring the inward immoral reality revealed by their speech and other behaviors? What are some of these examples? Discuss how you think the example of Jesus can help you respond to such people.

2. Jesus' response to Peter's plea for Jesus to avoid arrest and execution was to identify it as satanic (16:23). Compare Satan's proposal in 4:5–6 to Peter's plea in 16:22. Do you see any similarities? How did Jesus view Satan's enticement (4:7)? Compare that to Jesus' response to Peter (16:23). Do you think Jesus saw Peter's plea for Jesus to avoid the suffering and death that was to come as a test of his faithfulness to carry out the Father's will for him? Explain your answer.

3. Imagine you were one of Jesus' early disciples and you heard him talk about his upcoming arrest, execution, and resurrection. The only notion of resurrection you knew about was a general resurrection at the end of history. Based on Old Testament teaching (Ezekiel 37; Isaiah 26:19; Daniel 12:2), the Jews of Jesus' day believed in the resurrection of all the dead at the final judgment. This is why his disciples could not at first comprehend his teaching about his rising from the dead before the day of judgment (Mark 9:9–10; John 2:18–22; 11:23–24; cf. Matthew 28:16–17; Luke 24:36–43). Given your doctrinal belief, what of Jesus' prediction would you focus on? How would that make you feel? Does this help you better understand the disciples' confusion and grief?

LESSON 10

Community and Rejection

(Matthew 18–23)

Every believer was faithfully devoted to
following the teachings of the apostles.
Their hearts were mutually linked to one
another, sharing communion and coming
together regularly for prayer. A deep sense
of holy awe swept over everyone, and
the apostles performed many miraculous
signs and wonders. All the believers were
in fellowship as one body, and they shared
with one another whatever they had. Out
of generosity they even sold their assets to
distribute the proceeds to those who were
in need among them. (Acts 2:42–45)

Whether you're from a small or big family, attend a little or
large church, or work with few or many coworkers, it can be
tough to get along with others. According to Acts 2, the early followers were "mutually linked," were "in fellowship," and "shared
with one another whatever they had." It sounds like they held it
together pretty well, though they weren't without their bumps and
bruises (see, for example, the account of Ananias and Sapphira in
Acts 5:1–11).

In preparation for a new community of believers who were to follow a kingdom realm lifestyle, Jesus gave some instruction, provided some community ground rules. And he also explained, by way of some parables, the nature of rejection in the kingdom realm.

Community

Greatness and Humility

In Matthew 18:1–4, Jesus redefines greatness: he brings a child over and relates that being "teachable," wide-eyed, and "humble" are requirements in the kingdom realm. He furthers the discussion in 19:13–15, 20:25–27, and 23:8–12. Read all of these passages and then answer the questions that follow.

- *How is what Jesus defines as humility in direct contrast to a worldly definition of greatness? And why did Jesus use a child as an example?*

- *Jesus sees servitude as the most honorable state for a person with a kingdom realm mindset. How did Jesus demonstrate the ultimate example of how to have the heart of a servant?*

- *Jesus doubles down in chapter 23. What is the reward for those who eschew titles and who seek humility and serve others?*

Handling Sin

Jesus talks about sin in Matthew 18:7–9, specifically how we are to confront and deal with our own sins. As well, he addresses the issue of being sinned against in verses 15–17.

- *What are we to do in confronting our own sin? Does Jesus really want us to cut off our own hand or foot? To pluck out our own eye? What's the goal in addressing the sin?*

- *How are we to confront someone who sins against us? What is the goal in that situation? And how often should we forgive (vv. 22–23)?*

Salvation

Jesus tells a story about a lost lamb that illustrates his claim that "The Son of Man has come to give life to all who are lost" (v. 11).

- *Retell the story in your own words (vv. 12–13).*

- *How does Jesus' wrap-up in verse 14 relate to his opening claim in verse 11?*

- *What does this parable tell you about God's love for us?*

Marriage

In Matthew 19:4–6, Jesus talks about the true intent for marriage, when challenged on divorce. For Jesus, marriage is about unity; it is a type, a representation of the relationship between Christ and his church (cf. Ephesians 5:22–33).

- *Why did Moses permit divorce (Matthew 19:9)?*

- *For Jesus, what is the exception for allowing divorce? Why do you think Jesus permits that exception?*

Eternal Life

When a wealthy young man approached Jesus about how to "obtain eternal life" (Matthew 19:16–24), Jesus told him to get rid of all his possessions and follow him.

- *Did Jesus really mean for the young man to do that? Explain your reasoning.*

- *What did Jesus mean when he said, "it's easier to stuff a heavy rope through the eye of a needle than it is for the wealthy to enter into God's kingdom realm" (v. 24)?*

- *What are some ways you can work to guard your heart against the desire for obtaining possessions?*

Generosity

The next story Jesus tells is meant to help us "understand the way heaven's kingdom operates" (20:1).

- *Read through the parable Jesus tells (vv. 2–15). What did you learn about God's generosity?*

- *Now read verse 16. What does this add to your understanding of God's generosity and grace?*

The Blind See

Before Jesus enters Jerusalem and spends his final days of his earthly ministry, two blind men call out to him for healing. They refer to him as "Son of David" (20:30–31), indicating their belief that he was the long-awaited Messiah (1:1). Jesus felt compassion for them and healed them. And this led the crowd of people who witnessed the miracle to praise God, and it inspired the two healed men to become followers of Jesus (20:34).

The faith of the two blind men outside of Jerusalem serves as a contrast to what Jesus later experienced inside of Jerusalem's walls. There the religious leaders continue to try to trap him and eventually find a way to have him executed. What the blind men understood about Jesus even before they were healed was clear and accurate. The religious leaders, on the other hand, were hardened and blind to seeing Jesus for who he was: the Anointed Messiah.

Rejection

After his celebrated entry into Jerusalem and after he cleared the temple of "the money changers and the stands of those selling doves" (Matthew 21:1–10, 12–13), the religious leaders once again questioned Jesus' authority.

- *What question did the "leading priests and Jewish elders" pose to Jesus (v. 23)?*

- *Jesus responded with a question of his own, saying that he would answer their question if they first answered his. What was Jesus' question (v. 25)?*

- *What dilemma did Jesus' question pose for the religious leaders, and did they resolve it (vv. 26–27)?*

- *Did Jesus, then, answer their original question (v. 27)?*

ⓒ DIGGING DEEPER

Once again, Jesus used logic in his confrontation with the religious leaders. His question to them was a disjunctive dilemma. A disjunctive question is an either/or question; it has the form, "Is A true or B true?" The question compels an answer, and when it contains a dilemma where either option puts the recipient in a difficult position, it's particularly difficult to answer. In the case with the religious leaders, they recognized that Jesus had them in a corner. If they answered that John the Baptizer's authority came from heaven, then the people witnessing the encounter would ask why their leaders had not accepted John's teaching (v. 26). If, on the other hand, the religious leaders said that John's authority was not from God, then the people would be upset with them and mob them, for the people were "convinced that John was God's prophet" (v. 26). So the religious leaders chose to voice ignorance rather than find themselves hanging on one of the horns of the dilemma. Was this a better option for them? Imagine if authorities you looked up to claimed ignorance about something they should understand. Would you continue to trust that they knew what they were talking about? Your trust in them would at least be lessened.

These religious leaders had rejected John's message about repentance and the Messiah, and now they had the Messiah standing right in front of them, and they didn't recognize him. Instead they demanded that he reveal to them the authority upon which he carried on his ministry of teaching, healing, and exorcising demons. Jesus' response was to show that they were incompetent to judge his credentials, much less John's. And by posing a disjunctive dilemma to them, he gave them the opportunity to come clean about their true beliefs and assessments. But rather than unveil their unbelief, they hid behind a claim of ignorance, more afraid of the people and how they would look in their eyes than fearing the One they claimed to represent.

Parables about Rejection

Jesus continued to respond to his critics by telling three parables.

In the parable of the two sons (vv. 28–32), Jesus tells the story of one son who tells his father he won't work but then does anyway and another son who says he will work but then doesn't.

- *Which son do Jesus' detractors say did his father's will?*

- *Why did Jesus agree with them?*

The parable of the rejected son is a sad tale (vv. 33–41). An honorable man sets up a vineyard and leases it out. He sends his servants to collect the money he is owed at harvest time. The tenants beat, stone, and even kill his servants. The vineyard owner ends up sending his son, whom the tenants kill as well. It should be pretty obvious that Jesus is talking about himself and the Jewish leaders who are seeking to, and eventually do, kill him. According to verses 45–46, they realize this as well.

- *In verse 43, Jesus says the kingdom realm will be taken from the religious leaders seeking his destruction and "given to a people who will bear its fruit." Whom do you think Jesus is talking about? How can you be certain that you will inherit the kingdom and bear fruit?*

Read Matthew 22:1–14 about the parable of the wedding feast. Then answer the following questions.

- *What is the significance of this parable's setting being a wedding celebration?*

- *What did the king do when none of the invited guests accepted his invitation?*

- *What happened to the guest who didn't put on the clothing provided to him? Why? Does that seem a bit harsh to you? How does his treatment reflect the reality of the kingdom realm of God?*

🫀 EXPERIENCE GOD'S HEART

It is not God's heart to see his children rejected. Jesus knew this quite well, as he was rejected by his family (John 7:5), his hometown (Matthew 13:57–58), some of his closest friends (Judas and Peter), and even his heavenly Father (Matthew 27:46).

- *How did Jesus deal with rejection in each of the instances listed above?*

    Family

    Hometown

    Close Friends

    Heavenly Father

Jesus redeemed us. He bought us back, accepted us, and chose us. Jesus was not deterred by rejection, and we shouldn't be either.

- *How did Jesus redeem us? Read Romans 8:15. What is the "Spirit of full acceptance"?*

- *How can we overcome the rejection of other people, especially when they reject us because of Jesus?*

💜 SHARE GOD'S HEART

- *Do you know someone who feels rejected? How can you let this person know that they are not alone? How can you relate to this person? Maybe you've experienced something similar. Maybe you can simply be a nonjudgmental listener. Remind this person that he or she is a son or daughter of a loving Father, a Father who is in heaven and is waiting to adopt them as a son or daughter.*

What Is Due

Once again, Jesus' critics try to "entrap Jesus with his own words" (Matthew 22:15). So they strive to flatter him so as to pressure him to answer them (v. 16). They then ask Jesus a question in the form of a disjunctive dilemma (either/or): "Is it proper for us Jews to pay taxes to Caesar or not?" They think they have Jesus on the horns of a dilemma. If Jesus agrees that the Jews should pay their Roman taxes, then he will lose support among most of the people who see the Romans as oppressors and the Messiah as the one who will deliver them from the Romans. If, however, Jesus says that the Jews should not pay their Roman taxes, then Jesus becomes a rebel to the Roman state, and rebels were treated harshly, even executed, by their Roman overlords. So what option would Jesus take?

- *What did Jesus say to his critics about their true intentions to pose such a question (v. 18)?*

- *Review Jesus' answer to his critics' question (vv. 19–21). Did Jesus accept one of his critics' options? Or did he come up with a third alternative? Explain your answer.*

- *How did Jesus' critics respond to Jesus' answer (v. 22)?*

Clarity on the Resurrection

Another set of Jesus' critics, the Sadducees, tried to trap Jesus too. Even though they disbelieved in the resurrection of the dead, they presented Jesus with a hypothetical situation designed, they thought, to reduce the traditional (biblical) understanding of bodily resurrection to an absurdity (*reductio ad absurdum*; vv. 23–28). As Dallas Willard explains:

> The law of Moses said that if a married man died without children, the next eldest brother should make the widow his wife, and any children they had would inherit the line of the older brother. In the "thought experiment" of the Sadducees, the elder of seven sons died without children from his wife, the next eldest married her and also died without children from her, and the next eldest did the same, and so on through all seven brothers. Then the wife died (small wonder!). The presumed absurdity in the case was that in the resurrection she would be the wife of all of them, which was assumed to be an impossibility in the nature of marriage.

Jesus' reply is to point out that those resurrected will not have mortal bodies suited for sexual relations, marriage and reproduction. They will have bodies like angels do now, bodies of undying stuff. The idea of resurrection must not be taken crudely. Thus he undermines the assumption of the Sadducees that any "resurrection" must involve the body and its life continuing *exactly as it does now*. So the supposed impossibility of the woman being in conjugal relations with all seven brothers is not required by resurrection.[36]

But Jesus wasn't done with his answer yet. Having shown that the Sadducees' argument was flawed, that it did *not* reduce the doctrine of the bodily resurrection to an absurdity, Jesus then shifted to the very nature of God to establish that life after death had to be true—a position the Sadducees had rejected.

- *Read verses 31–32 and study note 'g' for verse 32. From the fact that God is the living God and the God of Abraham, Isaac, and Jacob—all ancient forefathers of the Jews—how is it that God can keep his everlasting covenant with these forefathers and they continue being in relationship with him if they are dead and buried and not alive in any sense? "One cannot very well imagine the living God communing with a dead body or a non-existent person and keeping covenant faithfulness with them."[37]*

- *If God can preserve a person's life through the physical death of the body, is it really out of God's reach to raise a dead body to life, transform it, and reunite it with the living person who once resided in it? Explain your answer.*

The Centrality of Love

A true community of Jesus' followers, those who seek a kingdom realm lifestyle, have to demonstrate love. As Jesus said: "Love the Lord your God with every passion of your heart...You must love your friend in the same way you love yourself" (Matthew 22:37–38).

- *What is the relationship between loving God, loving our friends and neighbors, and loving ourselves?*

- *What's the significance to Jesus explaining the "greatest commandment" in response to an attempt at being trapped by some religious leaders?*

Whose Son?

After Jesus' critics had been stunned and silenced by his answers, Jesus took the opportunity to ask a group of them his own question (v. 41).

- *What did Jesus ask, and what did the Pharisees answer (v. 42)?*

- *Jesus, then, quoted Psalm 110:1, a passage that his hearers accepted as a reference to the Messiah. Turn to Psalm 110 and read it, observing who wrote this psalm. Then answer the questions that follow:*

    Since King David wrote Psalm 110 under the inspiration of the Holy Spirit, what must we conclude about the Author behind David? Who was it? Why does this matter?

    From the quote Jesus gives (Matthew 22:44–45), what question does Jesus pose?

Through his question, Jesus is presenting an apparent contradiction. David was just a man, and any children he had would have been just as human as he was. Since that's the case, how could David call his own son Lord—a title used in this context referring to deity— when his son was not divine but only human? See the problem? Can this apparent contradiction be solved? The Pharisees didn't know how to solve it (v. 46). Can you? Explain your answer. (Hint: there really is a solution, and it's provided in this endnote.[38] But before you read it, see if you can solve the problem on your own or perhaps with the help of someone you know.)

Talking It Out

1. In the parable of the wedding feast, the king sends his servants out into the streets, and many accept his invitation, "good and bad alike" (Matthew 22:10). That means some were worthy of the invitation and some were not. That means that being worthy in the kingdom realm has nothing to do with being good or bad. Discuss what makes one worthy in the kingdom realm of God. Is it enough to simply be willing to accept the invitation? Do we still have to meet some expectations once we accept the invite? Recall that one guest was thrown out of the feast because he did not put on the clothing that the king provided for him.

2. Mathew 23:13–36 lists "Seven Woes." List and describe each of them, including the evidence Jesus provides for each of his indictments. Remember, too, that Jesus has had several encounters with these religious leaders throughout his ministry. He knows these leaders, their teachings, and their practices quite well.

3. Do you think Jesus' case against his outspoken critics is justified? Explain your answer.

4. At the end of his pronouncement of woes, Jesus laments over Jerusalem (vv. 37–39). What does Jesus think and feel about those who reject him?

LESSON 11

The Olivet Discourse

(Matthew 24–25)

Matthew 24–25 is known as the Olivet Discourse, and its subject is the end times. Let's set the scene a bit. Jesus had just finished speaking to some religious leaders concerning judgment (the seven woes). As Jesus and his disciples leave the temple courts, Jesus prophesies its destruction, which probably freaks out his disciples a bit. So they ask Jesus to tell them about the last days. Jesus then describes a coming judgment and tells a series of parables to encourage his followers in the way they can best prepare for his second coming.

The Temple, Jerusalem, and the Last Days

Matthew 24:4–35 is Jesus' detailed answer to his disciples' question: "Tell us, when will these things happen? And what sign should we expect to signal your coming and the completion of this age?" (v. 3). First, he provides a general description: (1) the prevalence of rampant deception; (2) rumors of wars and nations going to war against one another; (3) the occurrence of natural disasters; and (4) the persecution of his followers. Then he discusses the details of his return. But before he predicts these future happenings, he tells them about an event that will occur that will shake Judaism to its core: the destruction of the temple in Jerusalem (vv. 1–2).

The Temple's Demise

At the heart of Jewish worship in Jesus' day was the temple in Jerusalem. There the sacrifices were performed, and the priests interceded on behalf of the people. This temple structure, however, was not the one that Solomon built (1 Kings 6). That one had been built around 953 BC, and it housed, among other things, the ark of the covenant that had resided in the tabernacle since the wilderness wanderings of the Hebrews after their exodus from Egyptian bondage (Exodus 25). In 586, Babylonian King Nebuchadnezzar looted and burned Solomon's Temple (2 Kings 25:9, 13–17) and exiled most of the Hebrews from their native land. Years later in 538, the Persian King Cyrus authorized the return of the Hebrews to their homeland and the reconstruction of the temple. That structure was completed around 515, but the ark and many of the other temple furnishings were never recovered. This second temple was "smaller than and inferior to Solomon's (Ezra 3:12)."[39] Even before Jesus' birth, King Herod began adding to this temple as well as renovating it. This work began around 19 BC but wasn't completed until around AD 64. When Jesus predicted this temple's demise, as beautiful as it already was, parts of the temple complex were still under construction.

Just two years after the temple's completion (AD 66), a Jewish rebellion began against Roman rule. In the year 70, the Roman response to the rebellion led to the utter destruction of the temple. It was never rebuilt. What Jesus said would happen to it did.[40]

Deception

After Jesus' prediction concerning the Jerusalem temple, the disciples were clearly anxious about what else was to happen, including the events surrounding Jesus' second coming (Matthew 24:3).

- *What was the first end-times sign that Jesus described (vv. 4–5)?*

- *How should believers respond to such deception?*

Violence

- *What was the next end-times sign that Jesus told his disciples about (vv. 6–7)?*

• *How are believers supposed to respond to this sign and why?*

Upheavals

• *Jesus also predicted other upheavals that would occur as signs of the last days. What are they (v. 7)?*

• *What else did Jesus say about these signs (v. 8)?*

- *What does his description of them as "birth pains" signify to you about what these events will lead to? In other words, does Jesus provide a hint of hope for a better future to come?*

Persecution

- *Yet another end-times sign Jesus provides is in verse 9. What is it, and why will it occur?*

- *What will be the consequences of the persecution Jesus predicts (vv. 10–12)?*

- *Why do you think these consequences will follow the persecution of believers?*

- *What positives does Jesus hold out for us to cling to (vv. 13–14)?*

Great Misery

In Matthew 24:15–22, Jesus also predicted "a time of great misery beyond the magnitude of anything the world has ever seen or ever will see" (v. 21)—a time prophesied in Daniel concerning "the Holy Place" and a "disgusting destroyer," an event so desperate for Jesus to call on those in Judah to "escape to... higher ground" (v. 16). While some scholars view Jesus' prediction here as referring to a still future fulfillment, others, such as D. A. Carson, view it as fulfilled during the Jewish rebellion that led up to and included the fall of the city of Jerusalem and the destruction of its temple.

• *What does Jesus say about this time period (vv. 15–21)?*

• *What mercy will God show during it (v. 22)*

Concerning this catastrophic time, Carson writes:

> An historian who witnessed the destruction
> of Jerusalem and the desecration of
> the Temple after a siege of four years,
> described the horror. The famine was so
> severe that mothers ate their children.
> Rival groups within the city slaughtered
> one another and desecrated the Temple
> long before the Roman troops breached
> the walls of the city. The entire populace
> was either slaughtered or sold into slavery
> and the city was burned and razed to the
> ground.

There have been massacres of
greater numbers in the sorry history of
the [human] race, but what destruction
has been as cruel, so totally destructive,
proportionally so ruinous as this? There
have been more extensive judgments on
the race—remember the Flood—but the fall
of Jerusalem remains in a class by itself,
if only because the distress was not only
proportionately complete, but prolonged
and ruthless.[41]

Elsewhere Carson adds: "There have been greater numbers of
deaths—six million in the Nazi death camps, mostly Jews, and an
estimated twenty million under Stalin—but never so high a per-
centage of a great city's population so thoroughly and painfully
exterminated and enslaved as during the Fall of Jerusalem."[42]

Because Christians knew about Jesus' prediction and believed
he was the Messiah, they obeyed his warning and left Jerusalem
either just before the siege of the city began or about mid-way
through it when the Romans still permitted people to leave.[43] They
got out before the worst came upon the city.

False Prophets and Messiahs

Among last-day events will be the rise of false prophets and
messianic impostors (vv. 23–26).

- *How should Christians relate to these deceivers
  (vv. 23–26)?*

- *In contrast to the claims of these deceivers, what does Jesus say his second coming will be like (vv. 27–31)?*

The Second Coming and Judgment

Still answering the disciples' question about the future, Jesus slowly turns from direct teaching about judgment and the second coming to parables. Let's focus on the rest of his direct teaching first, and then we'll consider his parables.

Didactic Teaching

- *Along with what Jesus has already said about his second coming and the events leading up to it, what assurance does he provide that his predictions will come about (vv. 32–35)?*

- *What does Jesus say about the exact time of his second coming (v. 36)? Who knows this information?*

- *To emphasize the need for people to prepare for his end-of-days return, Jesus talks about judgment that will precede it.*

  To what Old Testament event of judgment does he compare this time and what does he say about it (vv. 37–39)?

  When "the Son of Man appears" (v. 39), what will be the sign that judgment is occurring (vv. 40–41)?

  Why has Jesus relayed this information about his second coming (v. 42–44)?

Parables of Preparation

Jesus compares his return to the state of the world just before it was destroyed in Noah's day. Many will not realize the end is near and will not be living a lifestyle of preparation. So the question is how should Jesus' followers be living? What should their kingdom realm lifestyle look like, specifically with regard to being expectant of Jesus' return?

Matthew 24:45–51 details the parable in which a master punishes a wicked servant when he returns home to find that his servant was misusing his position and was unprepared for his master's return.

- *What were some of the actions that the evil servant took?*

- *How can we sometimes be like the evil servant?*

- *Are we always ready for the return of Jesus? What are some things that we do that keep us unprepared?*

- *What are the characteristics of the faithful servant (v. 45)?*

Another parable is about ten young women in charge of waiting for the return of a newly married couple (25:1–13). They were to wait outside with lamps at the ready. Five were adequately prepared, but five were not.

- *What happened to the five women who were unprepared?*

- *Would you have shared some of your oil with those who were unprepared? Why or why not?*

Jesus tells two additional parables in Matthew 25. The third parable Jesus tells in the Olivet Discourse relates a story of three servants and their use (and in some cases misuse) of their master's finances (25:14–30). And the final parable (vv. 31–46) explains that, in the end, the saved and the unsaved will be separated.

- *Just as in the case of the ten young virgins when the bridegroom didn't come when he was expected (vv. 1–12), we do not know when Jesus will return. What is the main lesson here (v. 13)? How are we to interact with the unprepared?*

- *In the parable about financial stewardship, the first two servants were both praised, even though one did better than the other (vv. 14–30). What does this tell you about what is most important to God?*

Return to Direct Teaching

Before Jesus ends his Olivet Discourse, he returns to direct teaching, and this time he focuses on the final judgment yet to come. Following his second coming, Jesus will sit in judgment on all human beings who have ever lived.

- *With regard to the sheep and the goats in verses 31–46, who are the sheep, and who are the goats?*

- *What is the difference between how the sheep and the goats are treated as they stand before Jesus? And how are their lifestyles different?*

- *What are the different ends of the sheep and the goats?*

- *Do you know in which group you will stand at the final judgment? How do you know?*

 EXPERIENCE GOD'S HEART

According to Matthew 24:36: "But of that [exact] day and hour no one knows, not even the angels of heaven, nor the Son [in His humanity], but the Father alone" (AMP).

- *Why wouldn't God want us to know the exact time of Jesus' return?*

- *How does God expect us to live, especially since we don't "know the day or the hour" of Jesus' return? Reread 24:36–51.*

♥ SHARE GOD'S HEART

We should prepare and be ready for the second coming of Jesus; however, it's not just about us! Remember, we have a mission to share the truth about God's kingdom realm.

- *Where in life can you invest your time or resources to make the greatest eternal impact?*

- *As followers of Jesus, we definitely have the responsibility to share the message that Jesus is coming back someday. Whom can you reach out to, if not today, this week?*

Talking It Out

1. Matthew 24:14 is a reminder that the followers of Jesus have a "joyful message" (9:35) of heaven's kingdom to proclaim worldwide; indeed, every nation will see a "demonstration of the reality of God." Discuss what you know about missions worldwide and what you have learned about how God has been revealing himself to those who need him. What does all of this tell you about God's love for the world?

2. While God's love is real, so is his justice. Judgment is about the justice of God being carried out. Judgment is not contrary to love; indifference is. And God definitely cares about who we become and what we do in our lives. Talk about God's justice and what it implies about him and us. Also consider Romans 3:1–30. What does this passage reveal about God's judgment on us and how Christ has paid the price for our deliverance from that judgment?

3. What did you learn that you didn't know before about the last days and Jesus' return? Did what Jesus say have an impact on you? If so, in what way(s)?

LESSON 12

The Ultimate Proof

(Matthew 26–28)

The ultimate proof that Jesus was the Messiah, that he was who he said he was, comes to a conclusion in the last three chapters of Matthew's Gospel. Matthew's narrative culminates in betrayal, arrest, denial, abandonment, and death. But it also involves innocence, celebration, and pure joy. In Matthew 26–28, Jesus is condemned and crucified. Then he defeats death, rises from the dead, and sends his followers on a great mission to spread his love to the entire world.

Jesus' Last Days

Complete the timeline that covers the events of Jesus' last days as Matthew details them. Then answer any corresponding questions.

- _____ , *the high priest, plots with* _____ *to have Jesus arrested and killed (26:1–5).*

   What did Jesus do to prepare his disciples for what was to come?

What restrictions did the religious leaders place on their plot against Jesus?

• _____ anoints Jesus with oil (vv. 6–13). *(Her name is not given here but elsewhere; see study note 'd' for vv. 6–7.)*

How did Jesus' disciples react to this act? Why?

For Jesus, what did this act represent, and why was it justified?

• *Jesus celebrated* _____ *with his disciples (vv. 17–25).*

Why did Jesus' "heart long" to celebrate the Passover with his closest disciples?

What announcement did Jesus make while they were eating?

- *Jesus instituted* _____ *while they ate (vv. 26–29).*

   Jesus instituted two acts for his followers to observe. This was the first. What is its significance (see 1 Corinthians 11:17–34)?

   The second act Jesus instituted was baptism. Read Matthew 28:19 and Romans 6:3–4. What does baptism represent for Jesus' followers?

- *Jesus predicts that* _____ *will deny him three times (Matthew 26:31–35, 69–74).*

   Did Peter believe Jesus' prediction? How did he react to what Jesus said?

*Did Peter eventually do just what Jesus said he would?
Do his actions after denying Jesus show sorrow and
repentance? Why or why not?*

• *Jesus prays in an orchard called* _____
  (26:36–46).

   *What happens to Peter, James, and John while Jesus is
   praying?*

   Describe Jesus' emotional state during this time.

   *What does Jesus ask God the Father for? Does he get
   what he asks for?*

- *Jesus is betrayed by _____ and arrested (26:47–56).*

  By whose authority was Jesus arrested?

  What miracle does Jesus perform while he is being arrested?

  What did Jesus' disciples do after he was arrested?

- *Jesus is condemned to death by _____, the chief priest (vv. 57–68).*

  Whom did Jesus face upon his arrest?

  Was the evidence brought against him by witnesses enough to convict him?

What finally led to a guilty verdict?

In order for the fatal charge to be legitimate, what would have to be true about Jesus? If he really was the Son of Man, was his claim blasphemous?

- _____ kills himself (27:3–10).

In contrast to Peter's reaction to his betrayal of Jesus, this man kills himself. Why do you think he did that? Do you think he was repentant over what he did?

What prophecy did his actions fulfill? Why do you feel this was significant?

- *The Roman governor _____ hears the case brought against Jesus and eventually condemns him to death (27:11–32).*

A subtle shift takes place regarding the charge against Jesus. In the religious court, the fatal charge is _____ (26:65–66). When the religious leaders bring Jesus before the gentile Roman governor, what do they appear to charge him with (27:11)? Why do you think they abandoned the original accusation?

What was Jesus' defense before the Roman governor?

What did the governor do to try to appease the crowd so he could release Jesus, and why did he take this action?

Why did the governor eventually give in to the demands of the crowd?

How was Jesus treated prior to his death? Why was his suffering necessary?

- *Jesus is crucified at a place called _____ (27:33–44).*

  What sign was placed above Jesus' head?

  What were some of the things that people said to Jesus as he was hanging on the cross?

- *Jesus spoke this phrase before he died: _____ _____ (vv. 45–55).*

  What is the significance of the veil in the "Holy of Holies" ripping in two?

  What other strange things happened right after Jesus died?

*What did a Roman military officer confess after Jesus'
death?*

Who else witnessed Jesus' crucifixion from a distance?

• *Who buried Jesus? _____*
  __ (vv. 57–66).

In what manner was Jesus buried?

*Why did the Roman governor order soldiers to guard
Jesus' tomb?*

- Which two women first saw Jesus alive (28:1–15)?

  _____ and _____ .

Who rolled away the stone that covered Jesus' tomb?

What did Jesus say to the two women who saw him alive?

What did the women do following their encounter with Jesus near the gravesite?

What story did the religious leaders concoct to explain Jesus' empty tomb?[44]

- In your own words, what is Jesus' "Great Commission" (28:16–20)? To whom did he give this charge?

☻ EXPERIENCE GOD'S HEART

Leading up to Jesus' death, Matthew points out that Jesus was innocent and righteous; see, for example, 26:59 and 27:24. This demonstrates that Jesus did not die for his sins but for the sins of others. Paul writes this in 2 Corinthians 5:21: "For God made the only one who did not know sin to become sin for us, so that we might become the righteousness of God through our union with him."

• *Why was it necessary for Jesus to be innocent (sinless) in order to atone for us?*

• *When Jesus died, he spoke out and said: "My God, My God, why have you deserted me?" (Matthew 27:46). Have you ever been accused of doing something you didn't do? How did that make you feel? How do you think Jesus felt in the last moments of death, knowing he was completely innocent while suffering a tortuous and disgraceful death?*

🖤 SHARE GOD'S HEART

The ultimate way that we can share God's heart is by following through with the mission that Jesus gives at the end of Matthew 28. This mission has become known as "The Great Commission." Jesus grants his followers his authority and exhorts his disciples, and us as his followers, to make disciples and baptize.

- *Why do you think Jesus included baptism in his commissioning of his followers? What do you think is the significance of baptism?*

- *Have you ever "discipled" anyone? Did your experience coming to know Jesus as your Lord and Savior involve being "discipled"? Share your experiences with someone.*

Talking It Out

1. From Jesus' birth to his eventual execution, various individuals and groups sought his arrest and death. Review these passages from Matthew: 2:1–8, 12–18; 12:14; 21:45–46; 26:1–5, 14–16, 47–49, 57–66. Whom does Matthew identify as those who wanted Jesus out of the way? Why did they want to end Jesus?

2. What does this tell you about the hostility that can be exercised toward Jesus' followers? Is the potential cost worth the risk of following him? Discuss your answer.

3. Jesus vindicated his full identity, the source of his miraculous power, his authoritative teaching, and his power over sin and death by rising bodily from the grave. His resurrection was at the center of the church's earliest proclamations regarding him. Look up the following passages and summarize what they say about Jesus' resurrection and what it reveals about him: Acts 2:22–36; 17:1–4; 1 Corinthians 15:1–8, 11–20. Note as well the high importance these passages place on this event. Do you believe in Jesus' resurrection? If so, why? If not, why?

4. Consider Jesus' words in the Great Commission. Do you have any experience in evangelizing, preaching, or teaching? How do you feel about sharing the gospel with others? Do you have any doubts or fears? If so, talk about how you might be able to effectively address them and work through them.

5. What did you learn through your study of Matthew's Gospel that will likely remain embedded in your mind and heart as you move forward in your life? Take some time now to ask God to water this seed of truth and help it grow and flourish for your sake and the sake of others who need Jesus.

Endnotes

1. Brian Simmons et al., "A Note to Readers," *The Passion Translation: The New Testament with Psalms, Proverbs, and Song of Songs* (Savage, MN: BroadStreet Publishing Group, 2020), ix.

2 Eusebius, *The Ecclesiastical History*, trans. Kirsopp Lake, Loeb Classical Library 153 (Cambridge, MA: Harvard University Press, 2001), 297.

3 While a full discussion of the "two-source theory" goes beyond the scope of this study guide, an accessible discussion of the date of Matthew's origin can be found by visiting www.datingthenewtestament.com, a website maintained by the well-known researcher and author Craig A. Davis, author of *Dating the Old Testament* (2007). Also see Donald Guthrie, *New Testament Introduction*, 4th ed. (Downers Grove, IL: InterVarsity Press, 1990), ch. 5, "The Synoptic Problem." The sources allegedly behind Matthew's Gospel are wrapped up in what scholars refer to as the synoptic problem, which notices and attempts to explain how Matthew, Mark, and Luke have so much material in common and yet show some divergences with one another. Guthrie fairly and accurately covers this discussion.

4   Thieleman J. van Braght, *Martyrs Mirrors of the Defenseless Christians,* trans. Joseph F. Sohm (Scottdale, PA: Herald Press, 1938), 92–93. See also William Steuart McBirnie, *The Search for the Twelve Apostles* (Wheaton, IL: Tyndale House, 1986), ch. 10.

5   Billy Graham, "True Repentance, Real Change," *Decision: The Evangelical Voice for Today*, December 1, 2006, https://decisionmagazine.com/true-repentance-real-change/.

6   D. A. Carson, "Matthew," in *The Expositor's Bible Commentary*, vol. 8, ed. Frank E. Gaebelein (Grand Rapids, MI: Zondervan Publishing House, 1984), 99. See also Matthew 3:2, note 'h,' TPT.

7   Matthew 3:1, note 'e,' TPT.

8   Glen H. Stassen and David P. Gushee, *Kingdom Ethics: Following Jesus in Contemporary Context* (Downers Grove, IL: IVP Academic, 2003), 11.

9   For an accessible and extensive discussion of the parallels between Matthew and Luke's accounts, please see Darrell L. Bock, "Lecture 3: The Sermon on the Mount and the Sermon on the Plain," *The Life of Christ* (class lecture, "Biblical Training"), https://www.biblicaltraining.org/transcriptions/lecture-3-sermon-mount-and-sermon-plain.

10   D. Martyn Lloyd-Jones, *Studies in the Sermon on the Mount* (Grand Rapids, MI: Wm. B. Eerdmans Publishing Company, 1976), 12.

11   Lloyd-Jones, *Studies in the Sermon on the Mount*, 13.

12   Dietrich Bonhoeffer, *The Cost of Discipleship* (New York: Touchstone, 1995), 107.

13   Stanley Hauerwas and William H. Willimon, *Resident Aliens: Life in the Christian Colony* (Nashville, TN: Abingdon Press, 2014), 83.

14   Matthew 5:3, note 'e,' TPT.

15   Kristene DiMarco, vocalist, "Take Courage," written by Kristene DiMarco, Jeremy Riddle, Joel Taylor, track 5, on *Starlight* (Redding, CA: Bethel Music), 2016.

16   Matthew Henry, *Matthew Henry's Commentary on the Whole Bible: Complete and Unabridged in One Volume* (Peabody, MA: Hendrickson Publishers, 1991), 1671.

17   Article available online: Jon Bloom, "Lay Aside the Weight of Perfection," *Desiring God*, June 9, 2017, https://www.desiringgod.org/articles/lay-aside-the-weight-of-perfection.

18   Bill Johnson and Mike Seth, *Here Comes Heaven: A Kid's Guide to God's Supernatural Power* (Shippensburg, PA: Destiny Image Publishers, Inc., 2007), 79.

19   Jonathan T. Pennington, *The Sermon on the Mount and Human Flourishing: A Theological Commentary* (Grand Rapids, MI: Baker Academic, 2017), 255.

20   Lloyd-Jones, *Studies in the Sermon on the Mount*, 456.

21   Philip Yancey, *The Jesus I Never Knew* (Grand Rapids, MI: Zondervan, 1995), 178.

22   Bill Johnson, "Healing," Bill Johnson Ministries, accessed April 13, 2021, https://bjm.org/core-values/healing/.

23   N. T. Wright, *Jesus and the Victory of God* (Minneapolis, MN: Fortress Press, 1996), 658.

24   For more on the first-century conception of the Messiah in Israel, see Richard L. Niswonger, *New Testament History* (Grand Rapids, MI: Zondervan, 1988), 74–76. F. F. Bruce provides a fuller discussion in his book *New Testament History* (Garden City, NY: Doubleday, 1969), ch. 10.

25   J. Ligon Duncan III, "Lord of the Sabbath," Reformed Theological Seminary, May 31, 2009, https://rts.edu/resources/lord-of-the-sabbath/#.

26   Dallas Willard, "Jesus the Logician," *The Best Christian Writing*, ed. John Wilson (New York: HarperCollins, 2000), 265.

27   Willard, "Jesus the Logician," 265–66.

28   To see Jesus' argument laid out in a logical structure and to learn more about the *reductio ad absurdum* fallacy, go to Steven B. Cowan and James S. Spiegel, *The Love of Wisdom: A Christian Introduction to Philosophy* (Nashville, TN: B&H, 2009), 24–25.

29   Flavius Josephus, *The Works of Flavius Josephus*, trans. William Whiston (Peabody, MA: Hendrickson), http://www.perseus.tufts.edu/hopper/text?doc=J.+BJ+2.117.

30   D. A. Carson, "Matthew," 353.

31   F. F. Bruce, *The Hard Sayings of Jesus* (Downers Grove, IL: InterVarsity Press, 1983), 111.

32   Carson, "Matthew," 355, 356.

33   Carson, "Matthew," 362.

34   Carson, "Matthew," 362.

35   Carson, "Matthew," 394.

36   Willard, "Jesus the Logician," 268.

37   Willard, "Jesus the Logician," 269.

38   Willard provides the solution: "The resolution intended
      by Jesus is that they [the Pharisees] should recognize
      the Messiah is not *simply* the son of David, but also of
      One higher than David, and that he is therefore king in
      a more inclusive sense than political head of the Jewish
      nation (Rev. 1:5). The promises to David therefore reach
      far beyond David, incorporating him and much more. This
      reinterpretation of David and the Messiah was a lesson
      learned and used well by the apostles and early disciples
      (see Acts 2:25–36, Hebrews 5:6, and Phil. 2:9–11)." Willard,
      "Jesus the Logician," 269–70.

39   "Temple," *Nelson's New Illustrated Bible Dictionary*, ed.
      Ronald F. Youngblood (Nashville, TN: Thomas Nelson,
      1995), 1233.

40   For more information about the Jerusalem temple in its
      three manifestations, see "Temple," *Nelson's New Illustrated
      Bible Dictionary*, 1230–38. For more about Herod's temple
      work, see Alan Millard, "Herod, the Great Builder," in
      Treasures from Bible Times (Belleville, MI: Lion, 1985),
      169–73. F. F. Bruce provides background on the temple's
      development and Jesus' life and ministry in relationship to
      the temple: F. F. Bruce, *Jesus and Paul: Places They Knew*
      (Nashville, TN: Thomas Nelson, 1983), 58–63.

41   D. A. Carson, *God with Us: Themes from Matthew* (Ventura, CA: Regal Books, 1985), 141–42.

42   Carson, "Matthew," 501.

43   Carson, "Matthew," 501.

44   Since the first century, various theories have been concocted to explain away Jesus' empty tomb and his appearances to eyewitnesses, but none of them have held sway for very long because the evidence against them and for Jesus' resurrection is too strong. For more on these theories and the evidence for Jesus rising bodily from the grave, here are two informative online resources: Justin Holcomb, "What Is the Proof and Evidence for the Resurrection of Jesus?," Christianity.com, March 19, 2021, https://www.christianity.com/jesus/death-and-resurrection/resurrection/what-proof-is-there-of-the-resurrection-of-jesus.html; and Gary R. Habermas's website, which is dedicated to Jesus' historicity and resurrection: http://www.garyhabermas.com/. Dr. Habermas is perhaps the world's most knowledgeable advocate for Jesus' resurrection. An excellent printed resource is *The Case for the Resurrection of Jesus*, by Gary R. Habermas and Michael R. Licona (Grand Rapids, MI: Kregel, 2004).